Student Guide for

Educational Research
Competencies for Analysis and Application
Third Edition

L.R. Gay

Merrill Publishing Company
A Bell & Howell Information Company
Columbus   Toronto   London   Melbourne

Published by Merrill Publishing Company
A Bell and Howell Information Company
Columbus, Ohio 43216

International Standard Book Number: 0-675-20507-7
Printed in the United States of America
    3 4 5 6 7 8 9-91 90 89

CONTENTS

PART ONE

INTRODUCTION

TASK 1-A

> Given a reprint of a research study, identify and briefly
> state:
>> (a) the problem (purpose of the study),
>> (b) the procedures,
>> (c) the method of analysis, and
>> (d) the major conclusions.

Beginning on the next page, six research reports are reprinted. Following each reprint, spaces are provided for listing the components required by Task 1-A. As a self-test, after you have studied Part One, select at least two of the reprints (any two that look interesting to you) and see if you can identify the components. If your responses match the Suggested Responses in the back of this book, you are ready for Task 1-A. If your responses differ greatly from the Suggested Responses, study the articles again until you see why you were in error and then select two other articles and repeat the process. If by some chance you incorrectly identify the components of all five research reports, see your instructor.

Meaning As a Factor in Predicting Spelling Difficulty

JOHN N. MANGIERI
University of South Carolina

R. SCOTT BALDWIN
University of Tulsa

Reprinted from The Journal of
Educational Research, 1979, 72
(5), 285-287, by permission.

ABSTRACT   This study was designed to assess whether knowing the meaning of a word facilitates one's ability to spell it. A total of 180 fourth, sixth, and eighth graders took four spelling tests and four multiple-choice vocabulary tests on a list of 100 words. Results of analysis showed that when the effects of word frequency, word length, and phoneme-grapheme regularity were partialed out, there was still a significant relationship between ability to spell words and understanding of their meanings. Implications for the teaching of spelling and vocabulary are discussed.

During the past sixty years, tremendous energies have been focused on educational dilemmas associated with the teaching of spelling. Research has ranged from studies comparing instructional approaches (12, 14) to complex computer analyses of English orthography (10, 18). Primarily, spelling research can be subsumed under one of three headings: (a) characteristics of spellers, (b) methods of spelling instruction, or (c) properties of spelling words (6). The latter is the subject of the present investigation.

In their attempts to explain why some words are more difficult to spell than others, researchers have consistently observed moderate to strong relationships between spelling difficulty and (a) frequency of word occurrence, (b) word length (number of letters), and (c) extent of phoneme-grapheme regularity (5, 6, 11). Presumably, frequency of occurrence represents opportunity to learn, e.g., through reading; greater word length indicates increased opportunity for spelling error; and extent of phoneme-grapheme regularity suggests the degree to which a word may be spelled properly on the basis of sound alone.

In contrast to the previously cited factors, a minimal amount of research has attempted to assess the relationship between meaning and spelling. Does knowing the meaning of a given word facilitate its spelling?

Early studies of spelling ability (13, 15), as well as literature reviews focusing on spelling (2, 8, 16), emphasized the importance of word meaning in spelling instruction. More recently, Bloomer (4) found that words tend to be easier to spell if they have multiple meanings.

As long ago as 1922, Gates (9) observed high correlations between vocabulary knowledge and spelling ability. However, it is possible that a simple correlation between knowing what a word means and knowing how to spell it reflects a spurious relationship. This follows from the fact that words which children or adults are less likely to know the meanings of also happen to be those words which tend to be long in length and appear infrequently in printed matter.

The purpose of the present investigation was to determine whether or not understanding the meanings of words uniquely contributes to their "spellability," after the effects of word frequency, word length, and phoneme-grapheme regularity have been statistically partialed out.

Method

A total of 180 children—fifty-seven, sixty-six, and fifty-seven fourth, sixth, and eighth graders, respectively—served as the population for the study. Classes in which the children were tested provided a heterogeneous mix of high, average, and low achieving students. The subjects may be described as white and belonging to middle socio-economic levels.

Materials

One hundred words were randomly selected from *The Teacher's Word Book of 30,000 Words* (17). Frequency of occurrence in written materials, number of letters, and index of phoneme-grapheme regularity were calculated for each of the 100 words. Word frequencies were derived from the *American Heritage Word Frequency Dictionary* (7). The standard frequency index (SFI) was used. Essentially, the SFI is a $\log_{10}$ transformation of each word's estimated frequency per million tokens.

The index of phoneme-grapheme regularity was employed to provide a rough estimate of the probability of spelling an entire word correctly given no knowledge of the word other than the sequence of phonemes which comprises it. Each index was calculated in the following manner:

1. The pronunciation of each word was located in *Webster's Seventh New Collegiate Dictionary* (19).
2. The probability of occurrence for each phoneme-grapheme correspondence according to position in syllable was found using Tables 13 and 14 in *Phoneme-grapheme Correspondences as Cues to Spelling Improvement* (10).
3. The geometric mean of the phoneme-grapheme probabilities for each word was computed.
4. A $\log_{10}$ transformation was performed on the geometric means to reduce the extreme variability among the indices.

Procedure

The list of 100 words was broken down into sublists of twenty-five words each. Each sublist served as the basis for one vocabulary test.

The spelling tests were administered to subjects on four consecutive days. An oral dictation-in-context format was used. The multiple-choice vocabulary tests were also given on four consecutive days. Each vocabulary word was underlined, presented in a limited written context, and was followed by five possible answers. For example,

A *chapter* is part of (A) bridge (B) room (C) building (D) book (E) glossary.

Subjects were instructed to circle the letter of the correct answer. The number of times each of the 100 words was misspelled or assigned the wrong meaning was used as the index of the word's "spellability" and probability of bearing meaning for the subjects, respectively.

Statistical Design

Word frequency (WF), word length (WL), index of phoneme-grapheme regularity (P-GR), and index of word understanding (IWU) were entered into a forward stepwise multiple regression to predict the spelling difficulty (SD) of each word. Partial correlation coefficients were calculated between SD and each of the predictor variables, holding all other variables constant. Separate multiple regressions were also done using spelling and vocabulary data obtained from subjects at each level.

Results

The results of the stepwise regression which combined data from all grade levels are summarized in Tables 1, 2, and 3.

The obtained multiple correlation was .73 ($p < .01$), with WF, WL, IWU, and P-GR entering into the equation in that order. The regression equation is as follows:

$$\hat{Y} = .941 + (-.255WF) + .108WL + .241WU + (-.176P\text{-}GR)$$

The partial correlation between SD and IWU was .25

Table 1.—Simple Correlations between Spelling Difficulty, Word Frequency, Word Length, Word Understanding, and Phoneme-Grapheme Regularity

	WF	WL	IWU	P-GR
SD	-.58	.57	.55	-.35
WF		-.34	-.57	.20
WL			.44	-.39
IWU				-.03

$r.05 = .195$

Table 2.—Summary Statistics for the Stepwise Regression

Variable	Multiple-R	R^2	B
WF	.576	.332	-.255
WL	.699	.489	.108
IWU	.714	.510	.240
P-GR	.731	.534	-.176
Constant			-.941

($p < .01$). When the effects of WF, WL, and P-GR were partialed-out, there was still a significant relationship between subject ability to spell words and subject ability to identify the meanings of those words correctly.

Separate multiple regressions using spelling and vocabulary data from the fourth, sixth, and eighth graders yielded multiple-R's of .75, .71, and 165, respectively. Apparently, the predictability of spelling error has decreased at successive grade levels.

Discussion

The results of the present study indicate that there is a relationship between the spelling difficulty of a word and knowledge of the word's meaning. When subjects were unable to match words with appropriate meanings, they tended to misspell those words. The fact that this tendency remained after the effects of word frequency,

Table 3.—Partial Correlation Coefficients

	WF	WL	IWU	P-GR
SD	-.339*	.331*	.253*	-.22**

*$p < .01$
**$p < .05$

3

word length, and phoneme-grapheme regularity were eliminated suggests that the observed relationship between spelling difficulty and word meaning is not spurious.

In the authors' opinion, current practices in spelling instruction are characterized by isolationism. That is, good spelling has been viewed as a goal which is separate from other aspects of the language arts curriculum, e.g., vocabulary development. This has resulted in an unfortunately common pattern of spelling performance: students memorize and then spell words correctly for Friday's test, but are unable to spell those same words on Monday.

In view of the link between word meaning and spelling, the authors contend that students more proficient in spelling ability can be produced if the factor of meaning is integrated into spelling instruction. A combined spelling/ vocabulary approach is logical because words which are not understood cannot be used in writing. Hence, there is no need to know how to spell them. In the reverse case, understanding the meanings of words without knowing how to spell them impairs the clarity of writing.

In addition, it is possible that expressive competence, as it relates to individual words, is partially a consequence of the number of functional associations surrounding a word. The visual and auditory shapes, denotations, and connotations of a word may be mutually reinforcing, i.e., knowing what a word means may facilitate recall of its visual or auditory shape, and knowing what a word looks and sounds like may facilitate access to its meanings.

Spelling instruction is a logical extension of vocabulary acquisition and should be treated accordingly. Students should never be required to learn to spell words which they do not understand. When new vocabulary words are introduced, vocabulary and spelling instruction should proceed in tandem.

REFERENCES

1. Allen D., and Agers, J. "A Factor Analytic Study of the Ability to Spell." *Educational and Psychological Measurements,* 25 (1965):153-161.
2. Betts, E.A. "Inter-relationship of Reading and Spelling." *The Elementary English Review* 22 (1945):12-23.
3. Black, J.W. "Accompaniments of Word Intelligibility." *Journal of Speech and Hearing Disorders* 7 (1952):409-418.
4. Bloomer, R.H. "Concepts of Meaning and the Reading and Spelling Difficulty of Words." *Journal of Educational Research* 54 (1961):178-182.
5. Bloomer, R.H. "Some Formulae for Predicting Spelling Difficulty." *The Journal of Educational Research* 57 (1964):395-401.
6. Cahen, L.S.; Craun, M.J.; and Johnson, S.K. "Spelling Difficulty—A Survey of the Research." *Review of Educational Research* 41 (1971): 281-301.
7. Carroll, J.B.; Davies, P.; and Richman, B. (eds.). *The American Heritage Word Frequency Book.* New York: American Heritage Publishing Co., Inc., 1971.
8. Foran, T.G. *The Psychology and Teaching of Spelling.* Washington D.C.: The Catholic Education Press, 1934.
9. Gates, A.I. *Psychology of Reading and Spelling with Special Reference to Disability.* Contributions to Education, No. 129. Teachers College, Columbia University, 1922.
10. Hanna, P.R.; Hanna, J.S.; Hodges, R.E.; and Rudorf, E.H. *Phoneme-grapheme Correspondences as Cues to Spelling Improvement.* Washington: U.S. Government Printing Office, 1966.
11. Horn, T.D. "Spelling." In *Encyclopedia of Educational Research,* 4th ed., edited by Chester W. Harris, pp. 1282-1289. New York: MacMillan, 1969.
12. Mason, G.; McDaniel, H.; and Callaway, B. "Relating Reading and Spelling: A Comparison of Methods." *The Elementary School Journal* 74 (1974):381-386.
13. Reed, H.B. *Psychology of Elementary School Subjects.* New York: Ginn, 1938.
14. Reid, H.C. "Evaluating Five Methods of Teaching Spelling—Second and Third Graders." *Instructor* 75 (1966):77-82.
15. Russell, D.H. "Spelling Ability in Relation to Reading and Vocabulary Achievements." *The Elementary English Review* 23 (1946): 32-37.
16. Spache, G. "Spelling Disability Correlates I—Factors Probably Causal in Spelling Disability." *Journal of Education Research* 34 (1941); 561-586.
17. Thorndike, E.L., and Lorge, I. *The Teacher's Word Book of 30,000 Words.* New York: Teachers College, 1944.
18. Venezky, R.L. "English Orthography: Its Graphical Structure and Its Relation to Sound." *Reading Research Quarterly* 2 (1967):75-105.
19. Gove, P.B. (ed.) *Webster's Seventh New Collegiate Dictionary.* Springfield, Mass.: G. & C. Merriam Company, 1965.

SELF-TEST FOR TASK 1-A

Meaning as a Factor in Predicting Spelling Difficulty

The Problem

_____

_____

_____

The Procedures

_____

_____

_____

_____

_____

_____

The Method of Analysis

_____

_____

_____

The Major Conclusion(s)

_____

_____

_____

The Effect of Male Teachers on the Academic Achievement of Father-Absent Sixth Grade Boys

LEO M. SCHELL
DAN COURTNEY
Kansas State University

Reprinted from the Journal of Educational Research, 1979, 72 (4), 194-196, by permission.

ABSTRACT

Previous research has shown that as a group the reading achievement of father-absent elementary school boys is very low. It has been hypothesized that these boys might benefit from instruction by a male teacher. This study investigated whether assigning father-absent sixth grade boys to male teachers would result in higher academic achievement than that of similar boys assigned to female teachers, holding fifth grade achievement test scores and intelligence quotients statistically constant. Results indicated that male teachers had no significant effect upon the academic achievement of these boys. It is suggested that strategies other than assignment to male teachers be pursued by educators committed to helping improve the academic achievement of these boys.

BOYS WHOSE FATHERS ARE ABSENT for one reason or another (death, separation, divorce, etc.) comprise a disproportionate number of low academic achievers (3, 7, 8). One of the reasons frequently hypothesized for the relationship of father absence to poor academic achievement of the sons is the lack of an adult male figure who positively models academic activities, i.e., adult males who read in the presence of, and to, their sons and who reinforce imitative behaviors (3, 7, 8). Lacking an appropriate male model, the father-absent boy may not be motivated to achieve in these areas. The lack of an available father figure who will reward management behaviors required in school, i.e., sitting down when told, listening, following directions, etc., may indirectly contribute also to lowered academic achievement.

Blanchard and Biller (4) compared four groups of third grade boys on *Stanford Achievement Test* scores and teacher grades. The groups consisted of boys with a high amount of father interaction, those with a low amount of father interaction, early father-absent boys (before age five), and later father-absent boys (after age five). The father-absent groups scored below grade level, with the early father-absent group making lower scores than the other three groups. Santrock and Wohlford (12) found that father loss between ages six and nine had a particularly negative effect on academic achievement.

It has been argued that increasing the number of male teachers might "masculinize" the school culture and indirectly contribute to improved academic achievement of boys. This has been studied indirectly by comparing achievement of boys and girls in countries where there is a predominance of male teachers in the elementary school. In three studies, one in Germany (11), one in the United States, Canada, England, and Nigeria (10), and one in Japan (9), boys' achievement was higher where a majority of the teachers were men.

Asher and Gottman (1), however, found that the sex of the teacher was not a significant factor in the reading achievement of fifth grade students in the midwestern United States. None of these studies, however, specifically examined the achievement of father-absent boys under female and male teachers.

Brophy and Good (6), after reviewing the research, suggest that male teachers may be particularly helpful for fatherless boys.

This study investigated the effects of male teachers on the academic achievement of father-absent sixth grade boys. This grade level was chosen because it was the earliest level at which there was a large enough number of male teachers and where prior standardized achievement and intelligence test scores were available.

Method

Subjects

In a large midwestern city, 193 boys on whom there were complete data were identified from school records as being father absent. Of these, 90 had been assigned to 40 male teachers during their sixth grade year and 103 had been assigned to 46 female teachers, all in essentially self-contained classrooms.

Measure

Five total subtest scores from the *Iowa Test of Basic Skills*—Vocabulary, Reading Comprehension, Language, Work Study, and Mathematics—served as both the pretest and posttest measures, having been administered in April of the fifth and sixth grade years. Intelligence quotients were from the total score of the *Short Form Test of Academic Aptitude* (13), which had been administered in April of the boys' fifth grade year.

Table 1.—Analysis of Covariance with I.Q. and Fifth Grade *ITBS* Scores as Covariates

Source	df	Vocabulary Total		Reading Total		Language Total		Work-Study Total		Mathematics Total	
		MS	F	MS	F	MS	F	MS	F	MS	F
Covariate Pretests	1	65.36	.270	77.41	.168	60.98	6.17*	60.08	.280	48.33	.016
I.Q.	1										
Sex	1										
Residual	189										

*p < .05

Procedure

t-test comparisons between the two groups were made on the five criterion measures of the *ITBS*, intelligence quotients, and chronological age. There were no significant differences on any of the *ITBS* scores nor on the chronological ages, but there was a significant difference (*p* < .01) between the mean intelligence quotients of the groups. The mean I.Q. for the boys assigned to female teachers (Group F) was 99.1, while those assigned to male teachers (Group M) was 94.1. Also, even though none of the differences between *ITBS* scores was statistically significant, Group F had higher mean scores on all five of them. Therefore, analysis of covariance with I.Q. and fifth grade *ITBS* scores as covariates was used to analyze the data.

Results

The results of the analysis of covariance for both Group F and Group M are shown in Table 1. None of the five adjusted mean scores favored boys assigned to male teachers. However, the total Language score was significantly in favor, at the .05 level, of the boys assigned to female teachers. There was no evidence that assignment of father-absent boys to male teachers, in and of itself, was able to enhance the academic achievement of these sixth grade boys.

Discussion

The results of this study seem to make it clear that it is unrealistic to assign upper grade elementary father-absent boys to male teachers with the expectation of improving their academic achievement more than what would occur if they were assigned to female teachers. The expressed hope of many educators that these boys would somehow identify with a male teacher, see school achievement as a masculine as well a feminine trait, and thus work harder and learn more, was not borne out in this study. Assignment of these boys to male teachers, in and of itself, does not seem sufficient to attain this goal. In fact, female teachers were more successful in teaching these boys those things measured by the Language subtest of the *ITBS* than were the male teachers.

Two possibly influential factors were not considered in this study: length of father-absence and availability of male models other than the father. However, what was studied seems to be within the general parameters upon which a school or a school district would base a policy. These other factors may help in assigning individual boys to particular teachers, but they seem unlikely to be considered in creating a general policy covering most father-absent boys.

Male teachers at earlier grades might possibly have a more positive effect on these boys' academic achievement than did the sixth grade teachers in this study. However, the possibility of large numbers of male teachers entering primary grades is unlikely. Therefore, educators who are sincerely interested in the academic growth of father-absent boys will have to devise a series of more activist intervention strategies beginning as early as identification is possible. Waiting until these boys are older and then merely assigning them to a male teacher probably will not help them academically any more than will assigning them to a female teacher. Numerous active intervention strategies on helping elementary school boys in general have been suggested by Austin (2), Bradley (5), and Trela (14). Interested educators should refer to these books.

REFERENCES

1. Asher, S. R., and Gottman, H. M. "Sex of Teacher and Reading Achievement." *Journal of Educational Psychology* 65 (1973): 168-171.
2. Austin, D. E.; Clark, V.; and Fitchett, G. W. *Reading Rights for Boys.* New York: Appleton-Century-Crofts, 1971.
3. Biller, H. B. "Paternal Deprivation, Cognitive Functioning, and the Feminized Classroom." In *Child Personality and Psychopathology: Current Topics,* edited by A. Davids, pp. 11-52. New York: John Wiley, 1974.
4. Blanchard, R. W., and Biller, H. B. "Father Availability and Academic Performance Among Third-Grade Boys." *Developmental Psychology* 4 (1971): 301-305.
5. Bradley, R. C. *The Role of the School in Driving Little Boys Sane.* Wolfe City, Texas: The University Press, 1976.
6. Brophy, J. E., and Good, T. L. *Teacher-Student Relationships, Causes, and Consequences.* New York: Holt, Rinehart, and Winston, 1974.
7. Herzog, E., and Sudia, C. E. *Boys in Fatherless Families.* Washington, D. C.: U. S. Department of Health, Education and Welfare, Office of Child Development, 1970.
8. Hetherington, E. M., and Deur, J. L. "The Effects of Father Absence on Child Development." *Young Children* 26 (1971): 233-248.
9. Janis, I. L. *Personality Dynamics, Development, and Assessment.* New York: Harcourt, Brace and World, 1969.

10. Johnson, D. "Sex Differences in Reading Across Cultures." *Reading Research Quarterly* 9 (1973-74): 67-86.

11. Preston, R. "Reading Achievement of German and American Children." *School and Society* 90 (1962): 350-354.

12. Santrock, J. W., and Wohlford, P. "Effects of Father Absence: Influence of the Reason For and the Onset of the Absence." In *Proceedings of the 78th Annual Convention of the American Psychological Association*, pp. 265-266. Washington, D. C.: American Psychological Association, 1970.

13. Sullivan, E.; Clark, W. W.; and Tiegs, E. W. *Short Form Test of Academic Aptitude*. Monterey, Calif.: CTB/McGraw-Hill, 1970.

14. Trela, T. M. *Getting Boys to Read*. Belmont, Calif.: Fearon Publishers, 1974.

SELF-TEST FOR TASK 1-A

The Effect of Male Teachers on the Academic
Achievement of Father-Absent Sixth Grade Boys

The Problem
_____
_____
_____

The Procedures
_____
_____
_____
_____
_____
_____
_____

The Method of Analysis
_____
_____
_____

The Major Conclusion(s)
_____
_____
_____

Prestigious Psycho-Educational Research Published from 1910 to 1974: Types of Explanations, Focus, Authorship, and Other Concerns

CHARLES K. WEST
DEBRA GREEAR ROBINSON
University of Illinois
Urbana-Champaign

Reprinted from the Journal of Educational Research, 1980, 73 (5), 271-275, by permission.

ABSTRACT   Seventy-eight empirical articles were randomly selected from among articles published by the *American Educational Research Journal, The Journal of Educational Psychology*, and the *Journal of Educational Research* from the initial publication of these journals through 1974. Data were extracted from each article on types of explanation, type of study, focus, authorship, external funding, affiliation of authors, number and type of subjects, and references. Results indicate that almost one-half of the studies yielded descriptions rather than explanations. Most of the explanations were empirical, as opposed to vitalistic or teleological, generalizations.

This review is an attempt systematically to describe prestigious psycho-educational research published in selected journals from the first date of their publication to recent times. Unlike other reviews, which are topically focused, this review is focused on such concerns as the types of explanations generated, number and types of subjects, patterns of topics, and funding and institutional affiliations of authors.

Three journals were selected on the basis of two primary factors, citation frequency and rejection rate. Both the *Journal of Educational Psychology* (*JEP*) and the *Journal of Educational Research* (*JER*) have been found by Vockell and Asher (7) and White and White (11) to be cited frequently. More specifically, Vockell and Asher (7) found the *JEP* and the *JER* to be ranked first and second, respectively, among fifteen journals in number of citations. All three journals currently have a high rejection rate. In private correspondence, editors report a rejection rate of 88 percent in 1976 for the *JEP*, an estimated rejection rate between 80 percent and 90 percent during the past six years for the *American Educational Research Journal* (*AERJ*), and a rejection rate for the *JER* of 82 percent in 1977.

A secondary reason for selecting the *JEP* and the *AERJ* is that these journals are published, respectively, by the American Psychological Association and the American Educational Research Association, professional organizations with which educational psychologists are likely to be affiliated.

As Brown rightly notes, much of the controversy about the success and failure of the social sciences centers on the nature of the explanations they generate (2:40). Critics maintain that too many explanations offered by social scientists are vitalistic or teleological in nature. The criticism of vitalistic and teleological explanations is based on the idea that scientific explanations should allude to causes of behavior (in human psychology) outside the organism itself. The criticism appears invalid as more and more data accumulate to support the idea that human behavior is controlled by needs, purposes, motives, or other internal tendencies. A major problem with these explanations, however, and one that does suggest some validity to the criticism, comes from the perspective that explanations should ultimately lead to the control of the phenomenon being explained. Vitalistic and teleological explanations allow description and prediction, but they do not yield technologies of human control. Furthermore, most applied fields of psychology are at least partially, if not primarily, technological in orientation. In that sense, then, these explanations impede the expected flow from explanation to technology, and other types of explanations may be more valuable.

Such criticisms create a need for research into the kinds of explanations in fact offered by the social sciences. Yet, no empirical study to date could be located by the authors on the frequency of types of explanations in educational psychology.

Among the epistemological discussions on the nature and types of explanation, Brown's types seem to be the most applicable to educational psychology. So much of the literature on explanation and the nature of knowledge seems most appropriate for the physical sciences. Yet, though some explanatory issues and concerns are shared by the social and physical sciences, such issues are sufficiently distinct in the social sciences to warrant different categorical schemes. Brown developed his categories from the content of the social sciences, including psychology, and includes explanatory types such as intentions (aims, motives, purposes) and dispositions (personality, needs) among them. Furthermore, Brown's categorical scheme is more extensive than that of others, such as Fodor (4).

Several of Brown's types did not appear in the research examined and will not be defined or discussed. Also, by his own admission, his categories are not mutually exclusive. Brief definitions of Brown's (2) types of explanation found in this study may be helpful:

● *Descriptions*. Description is not really explanation. It is a recounting of events or characteristics of subjects. Example: The study seemed to indicate that second grade children have a more clear understanding of the past than they do of the present (5).
● *Intentions*. Intentional explanations are responses to "why" kinds of questions. They refer to subjects' aims, purposes, or motivations as controlling behavior. Example: Unless students attempt to improve their eye movements in reading they will not progress (8).
● *Dispositions*. Dispositional explanations generally employ personality variables, emotional states, or needs to explain behavior. Example: The personality of the student plays a more important role in scholarship than . . . (6).
● *Empirical Generalizations*. These are universal hypotheses asserted about relationships. They are based on observations and avoid abstraction or theoretical processes and states, especially intentions and dispositions. Examples: The use of defined words in sentences enhances learning (1). Programmed instruction reduces the time required to learn statistics (9). (For the purposes of this study, the term "learning" alluding to a dependent variable is considered to be based on observations, when appropriate measures of performance were made).

Method

Articles in the sample were drawn on the basis of half-decade periods beginning in 1910. The research articles in each volume were numbered according to the order of appearance. Computerized random numbers were generated to first select a volume of each journal and then an article from that volume. Replacement articles were chosen in the same fashion if nonempirical articles were initially selected. Three articles per half decade, per journal, were selected. The journals began publication at different times, so thirty-nine *JEP*, six *AERJ*, and thirty-three *JER* articles were analyzed.

Two judges independently selected the explanatory statements of each article from its summary or conclusion. The seventy-nine articles contained 195 statements characterized as explanatory, including descriptions. Explanations were categorized using Brown's types (2). Two judges independently categorized the explanatory statements into one of the categories and discussed to consensus the fifteen cases of disagreement. This and other data [number and description of subjects, author description (sex, coauthorship, affiliation), reference data, and so forth] were recorded on data summary sheets and then checked for accuracy.

Results and Discussion

Table 1 includes the basic data by decade and journal. In the first three columns the frequency of each type of explanation is given. Ninety descriptive explanations, nineteen intentional-dispositional, and eighty-six empirical generalizations were found. In the next several columns data on the type of study, experimental or nonexperimental, and focus of study are recorded. Only those studies that applied some treatment with seemingly appropriate control groups are designated as experimental.

Empirical generalizations were more typical of experimental studies than either descriptive or intentional-dispositional explanations, whereas descriptive and intentional-dispositional explanations were more frequently used in nonexperimental studies. Experimental studies yielded three descriptive, one intentional-dispositional, and thirty-five empirical generalization explanations. For the nonexperimental group eighty descriptive, eighteen intentional-dispositional, and forty-two empirical generalizations were found.

Studies during 1950 and after included more empirical generalizations and fewer of the other types of explanations than studies through 1949. For the period 1910-1949, sixty-four descriptive, fifteen intentional-dispositional, and thirty empirical generalizations were found. For the period after 1949 there were twenty-six descriptive, four intentional-dispositional, and fifty-six empirical generalizations. It is possible, then, to characterize the pre-1949 period as a descriptive era and the post-1949 period as an era of empirical generalization. Though there were more experimental studies and fewer nonexperimental studies in the more recent period, the difference is not great. One might have expected that the field had become a great deal more experimental, but evidently this was not the case.

Table 1.—Summary of Data on Type of Explanation, Type of Study, and Focus on Achievement

Decade & Journal	Type of Explanation			Type of Study		Focus on Achievement	
	Description	Intentional-Dispositional	Empirical Generalization	Experimental	Nonexperimental	Yes	No
1910-19							
JEP	8	5	4	2	4	14	3
1920-29							
JEP	6	2	4	1	5	7	5
JER	11	2	5	1	5	19	
1930-39							
JEP	11		8	3	3	15	5
JER	11	1	5	2	4	8	9
1940-49							
JEP	8	1	1		6	8	2
JER	9	4	3		6	12	4
1950-59							
JEP	3		8	1	5	6	5
JER	4	3	6	1	5	10	3
1960-69							
JEP	7	1	11	1	5	12	7
JER	3		9	3	3	6	6
AERJ	2		8	2	1	5	5
1970-74							
JEP	3		4	1	2	6	1
JER	3		4	2	1	5	2
AERJ	1		6	2	1	5	4
Totals	90	19	86	22	56	138	61

Intentional and dispositional explanations in modern times are largely used only by social scientists, but did not appear frequently in our sample. Intentional explanations are teleological: that is the present (current behavior) is explained in terms of the future (goals). Dispositional explanations are somewhat vitalistic in that some current "vital force" (needs, drives) within the subject is evoked to explain current and, perhaps, future behavior.

Returning to a discussion of Table 1 data, the majority of studies over the period focused on achievement—concerns such as predicting achievement, learning rate, minority group performance, and collegiate failure or success. The majority of the studies classified as nonachievement focused on such concerns as attitudes, self-concept, comprehension of time, and personality assessment.

In Table 2 data are presented on some miscellaneous variables. For example, according to the table, from 1910 to 1919 five articles of the sample chosen from the JEP were authored by individuals and one article had two authors. Single authorship, obviously was most characteristic over the entire period.

In the determination of the sex of authors, we relied on first names, a practice of course, subject to some error. Readers might be interested in the small number of female authors in the sample, as well as the fact that there are no cases of coauthorship in which females were first authors. There are seven articles in which the sole author is female.

The general pattern of author affiliation runs toward the college or university. The most representative institutions among the sample were the University of Illinois

Table 2.–Summary of Data on Number of Authors, Sex of Author, External Funding, Author Affiliation, and Mean Number of Subjects and References

Decade and Journal	Number of Authors				Sex of Author		Externally Funded		Author Affiliation		Mean Number of Subjects	Mean Number of References
	1	2	3	4	M	F	Yes	No	College or University	Other		
1910-19												
JEP	5	1			5	2		6	4	2	264	1.67
1920-29												
JEP	6				5	1		6	4	2	150	.67
JER	4	2			6	2		6	2	4	332	3.00
1930-39												
JEP	5	1			7			6	3	3	294	6.50
JER	4	2			8		1	5	5	1	297	3.33
1940-49												
JEP	4	2			7	1		6	5	1	123	3.50
JER	5	1			6	1	1	5	4	2	39,631	1.83
1950-59												
JEP	6				5	1	1	5	4	2	304	5.50
JER	6				6			6	5	1	300	5.50
1960-69												
JEP	2	3	1		10	1	2	4	6		290	8.00
JER	4	2			6	2		6	5	1	141	4.17
AERJ	2		1		5		2	1	2	1	281	5.67
1970-74												
JEP	1	1	1		4	2	2	1	3		194	6.33
JER	2	1			3	1		3	3		34	2.67
AERJ	2	2		1	8			3	3		293	8.00
Totals	56	18	3	1	91	14	9	69	58	20		

(six authors), Teachers College, Columbia University (four), University of Arkansas (two), Stanford (two), and Texas (two). These findings are somewhat similar to those of Cox and Catt (3) and West (10).

The data on numbers of subjects are interesting. The range of N is from 0 to 236,020. The studies having no subjects were conducted during the 1930s and used fake data to test various analyses. The smallest actual N is 8. Inspection of N means does not indicate that the advent of the computer resulted in larger N investigations, which may be surprising to some.

In regard to the types of subjects studies, forty-three studies involved college subjects, thirty-one involved college undergraduates, and five involved adults other than college undergraduates. The field is somewhat vulnerable to the criticism of the use of captive college students.

There does not seem to be any particular decade in which increasing numbers of references were used. One might have expected that as research accumulated over the decades more previous research would be cited. This may be mild evidence for the "face ignoring" (if not "face stepping") character of this social science, as opposed to the "shoulder standing" character of the natural sciences, to which Zeaman (12) humorously alluded. Regarding scholars referenced, no scholar was referenced more than three times. Those most frequently appearing were primarily statisticians as opposed to highly reputed theorists. This may suggest that a history of empirical educational psychology could be written with focuses other than "great ideas or theories developed by eminent persons." Perhaps statistical developments provide broader "shoulders" and are also relatively "faceless."

Conclusion

Educational psychology, as it is reflected in the sample, does not seem merely to be descriptive. Nor does the field seem dominated by teleological or vitalistic explanations. The major trend observed seems to be toward the use of empirical generalizations. Our study suggests that it is possible to characterize the period from 1910 through 1949 as a descriptive era. The period since then could be termed the era of the empirical generalization.

The vast and expanding amount of published research in most academic fields makes it increasingly difficult to determine the "state of the art" or obtain acceptable data on historic trends. It may be that the procedures used in this study suggest helpful paradigms for future historians of the social sciences.

NOTE

A list of references examined will be supplied on request to the first author.

REFERENCES

1. Anderson, R., and Kulhavy, R. "Learning Concepts from Definitions." *American Educational Research Journal* 9 (1972): 385-90.
2. Brown, R. *Explanation in Social Science*. Chicago: Aldine Publishing Company, 1963.
3. Cox, W. M., and Catt, V. "Productivity Ratings of Graduate Programs in Psychology Based on Publication in the Journals of the American Psychological Association." *American Psychologist* 32 (1977):793-813.
4. Fodor, J. A. "Functional Explanation in Psychology," In Brodbeck, M. *Readings in the Philosophy of Social Science*. London: MacMillan, 1968, pp. 223-38.
5. McAulay, J. D. "What Understandings Do Second Grade Children Have of Time Relationships?" *Journal of Educational Research* 54 (1961):312-14.
6. Miner, J. B. "The College Laggard." *Journal of Educational Psychology*. 1(1910):263-71.
7. Vockell, E., and Asher, Wm. "Critiques and Critical Comments in Educational Research Journals." *Educational Researcher* 1, no. 5 (May 1973):11-12.
8. Simpson, R. G. "Does the Amount of Free Reading Influence the Student's Control of His Eye Movements in Reading Ordinarily Printed Material?" *Journal of Educational Psychology* 34 (1943):313-15.
9. Smith, N. "The Teaching of Elementary Statistics by the Conventional Classroom Methods vs. the Method of Programmed Instruction," *Journal of Educational Research*, 55 (1962): 417-20.
10. West, C. K. "Productivity Ratings of Institutions Based on Publication in the Journals of the American Educational Research Association: 1970-76." *Educational Researcher*, February, 1978.
11. White, M. J. and White, K. G. "Citation Analysis of Psychology Journals." *American Psychologist*, 32 (1977):301-5.
12. Zeaman, David. "Skinners Theory of Teaching Machines." In *Automatic Teaching: The State of the Art*. Galanter, E. (Ed.). New York: John Wiley & Sons, Inc., 1959.

Prestigious Psycho-Educational Research Published From
1910 to 1974: Types of Explanations, Focus,
Authorship, and Other Concerns

The Problem

_____

_____

_____

The Procedures

_____

_____

_____

_____

_____

_____

_____

The Method of Analysis

_____

_____

_____

The Major Conclusion(s)

1910-1949 - descriptive era

1949-present - empiracal generalization.

_____

RESEARCH QUARTERLY
1979, Vol. 50, No. 3, pp. 328–332

Effects of Goal Setting on Achievement in Archery

MARY L. BARNETT AND JEAN A. STANICEK

This study investigated the effects of goal setting in teacher-led group conferences on achievement in archery. University undergraduates enrolled in three beginning archery classes ($N = 30$) were randomly assigned to two treatment groups—group conference with goal setting and group conferences only. For 10 weeks, subjects met twice a week for archery instruction and once a week with the instructor for a 10-minute conference. Subjects in the goal-setting conference group were directed to set numerical and verbal goals using a printed goal-setting form. Three achievement tests were administered while subjects were shooting from a distance of 20 yards: an initial test during week 1, a progress test during week 6, and a final test during week 10. Analysis of the data indicated that when groups were adjusted for initial differences, the goal-setting group achieved significantly higher scores in archery than the non-goal-setting group ($F = 5.31, p < .05$). Motivational implications of goal setting procedures are discussed.

The effects of goal setting on learning a gross motor task in the classroom recently have been studied by Barnett (1977) and Hollingsworth, (1975.) Both studies utilized a novel motor skill, juggling, in the existing instructional setting and neither found significant differences in achievement between goal-setting groups and groups having no specific goals. Both researchers suggested investigation of other tasks and use of longer learning periods. It is not known, for example, if goal setting would have an effect on learning and performance of a motor skill less novel than juggling and one which extended over the regularly scheduled instructional period.

There is ample evidence in the literature to indicate that performance goals are potent variables affecting behavior. Studies conducted in laboratory situations consistently have shown that subjects provided with experimenter-set "hard specific

Mary L. Barnett is an assistant professor in the Division of Health and Physical Education, Wayne State University, Detroit, MI 48202. Jean A. Stanicek, prior to her death in October 1978, was an associate professor in the Division of Health and Physical Education, Wayne State University.

goals" attain a higher level of performance than subjects told to "do your best" (Bryan & Locke, 1967; Locke & Bryan, 1966, 1967). Studies also have compared self-set goals to experimenter-set goals. A series of five studies by Locke, Bryan, and Kendall (1968) clearly indicates that self-set goals are superior to experimenter-set goals if the goals are appropriately difficult and specific. Recently, research has been reported that attempts to extend the goal-setting theory to more realistic tasks. Studies indicate that employee performance is enhanced by goal setting in a variety of organizational and industrial situations (Kim & Hamner, 1976; Latham & Baldes, 1975; Locke, 1968). Effects of participative goal setting in the organizational situation is. not as clear. A participative goal-setting condition led to higher productivity in uneducated workers in a study by Latham and Yukl (1975), while no difference was found between assigned and participative goal setting in another study (Latham & Yukl, 1976).

It is important to determine the effects of participative goal setting on performance in the classroom instructional situation as well. Evidence that student goal setting in classroom instructional situations leads to increased skill achievement is lacking. Participation in individual goal-setting conferences resulted in increased reading achievement in one of two grade levels studied by Gaa (1970). However, in a a similar study Marliave (1970) found that the reading achievement of students participating in goal-setting conferences did not differ significantly from that of a group having only a conference or a control group. The time requirements of the individual-conference goal-setting teachnique limit the usefulness of this approach for the typical classroom instructional situation. Some classroom goal-setting studies have been of short duration. Harvey (1971) sought to accomplish realistic goal setting in the group situation. The task involved identification of mistakes in a set of pictures illustrating the preparation of food. Subjects who were encouraged to set goals demonstrated a greater increase in the number of mistakes found from the first to the last picture than did control subjects. However, it is difficult to generalize the results of this short-term study (one class session) to the long-term tasks more common in education.

Barnett (1975) investigated the effects of goal setting in student-led small groups and in teacher-pupil conferences on the learning of a gross motor task —three-ball juggling. Female high school students ($N = 93$) were randomly assigned to five treatment groups: student-led interaction with goal setting, student interaction only, teacher-pupil conference with goal setting, teacher-pupil conference only, and control. The subjects practiced three-ball juggling in 16 practice and testing periods. The Trussell juggling achievement test was used. Subjects in the four experimental groups met weekly during the 3-week instructional period for structured interaction sessions or conferences. Subjects in the two goal-setting groups were directed to set specific numerical and verbal goals. There were no significant differences in juggling achievement among the five groups, either on the final test, or on a posttest administered to determine possible long-term effects. However, data collected in this study suggested that the nature of the task of juggling leads to goal setting by all subjects and that interest in the skill of juggling was high, as indicated by subjects reporting continued juggling activity after the conclusion of the study. Many motor skills included in regular instructional programs are not so novel. Perhaps directing students to set specific goals for skills where motivation is low can be an effective tool for increasing achievement. Perhaps a longer instructional period is necessary for goal-setting procedures to be effective in the classroom setting.

The purpose of the present research was to study the relationship of specific participative goal setting to achievement in archery over the regularly scheduled 10-week instructional period.

Procedures

Wayne State University undergraduates enrolled in 3 beginning archery classes were randomly assigned to one of two groups—group conference with goal setting or group conference only. Each group began with 20 students. However, some students withdrew voluntarily by their failure to attend instructional sessions, and data for others were incomplete (i.e., no score on any one or a combination of the three official tests), leaving a total of 30 subjects—18 in the group conference with goal setting group and 12 in the group conference only group.

Subjects in the group conference with goal setting group were directed to set individual verbal and numerical goals at the end of each weekly 10-minute conference period using a printed goal-setting sheet. Two different goal setting forms were prepared. The first included a list of verbal items the instructor felt important for early focus by students; it was used for the first half of the experimental period. The second, used during the second half of the experiment, incorporated more difficult verbal items while retaining those listed on the first form. In each case, verbal items were listed under the following categories: stance, nock, draw, aim, release, and follow through. Space was always provided for subjects to write their own verbal goals. Subjects were also directed to set a numerical goal for the week in terms of increase in score for any one end shot (six arrows).

The conference only group met weekly for 10 minutes with the instructor and discussed problem areas in the skill of archery. Those points listed as important for focus on the goal-setting sheet were introduced verbally to the conference only group. However, subjects were not specifically directed to set goals, either verbal or numerical, and were given no printed goal-setting sheets.

All subjects participated in the 10-week instructional unit in archery. Classes met twice a week for 50 minutes. Subjects were tested three times while shooting from a distance of 20 yards. The initial test took place during the first week of classes after minimal instruction and prior to any conferences or goal setting. The progress test was administered during the sixth week of classes, and the final achievement test during the tenth week. The initial performance score was the average of two ends, while the progress and final achievements scores for each subject were the averages of four ends. After the initial test from 20 yards, the instructor moved students to a distance of 10 yards to begin instruction and practice. Shooting distance was increased gradually during the first 5 weeks of the instructional period. All instruction and conferences were conducted by the same instructor.

Results and Discussion

Analysis of the performance score data was completed using a split-plot ANCOVA with initial test performance scores used as a covariate for the between-subject effect. The results of the data analysis indicated a significant group effect when adjusted for initial differences ($F_{1,27} = 5.31, p < .05$). Mean performance scores, standard deviations, and overall adjusted mean scores are shown in Table 1.

The adjusted mean of the conference with goal-setting group (37.05) was significantly higher than the adjusted mean (31.95) of the conference only group. There

Table 1—Means and Standard Deviations for Archery Achievement Tests

Group	Progress ($\bar{X} \pm SD$)	Final ($\bar{X} \pm SD$)	Overall ($\bar{X} \pm SD$)	Overall Adjusted ($\bar{X}$)
Experimental (n = 18)	32.97 ± 7.80	40.26 ± 6.49	36.61 ± 7.98	37.05
Control (n = 12)	33.18 ± 9.62	36.62 ± 9.14	34.90 ± 9.34	31.95
Overall	33.06 ± 8.41	38.80 ± 7.72		

was a significant effect of time, with the mean of the final test significantly higher than the mean of the progress test ($F_{1.28} = 35.65, p < .01$). There was no significant Group × Time interaction effect ($F_{1.28} = 3.85, p > .05$).

The findings support the conclusion that participative goal setting can be effective in promoting increased achievement in a motor skill—archery—when utilized over a 10-week instructional period. Subjects directed by the instructor during group conferences to set specific numerical and verbal goals, using a printed goal-setting form, had significantly higher archery scores than subjects participating in conferences with no specific goal setting.

The goal-setting procedure may have acted primarily to increase motivation and maintain task interest, since both goal-setting and non-goal-setting groups participated in instructor-led conferences in which problem areas involved in archery skill development were discussed. Evidence is available from laboratory research that specific performance goals can act to enhance interest in a task and that this effect on interest is greater with increasing length of the experiment and/or length of the trial period (Locke & Bryan, 1967). Examination of the group affiliation of those subjects dropped from the present study provides additional evidence that the goal-setting procedures may have acted to increase motivation and maintain interest in the task. Of the 40 subjects beginning the course, 10 were dropped from the study due to incomplete data; i.e., no score on one of the official tests or withdrawal from the class due to lack of attendance at instructional sessions. Both subjects dropped from the goal-setting group were dropped due to failure to attend one of the official testing sessions. One subject in the conference only group was dropped due to a missed class session which happened to fall on an official testing date. These three subjects continued in the course and received passing grades. The remaining seven subjects who were dropped from the study (all from the conference only group) had poor attendance and officially dropped the class. Thus, it appears that the goal-setting procedure acted to increase motivation and maintain task interest. It would be valuable in future studies of goal setting to formally assess motivation and interest.

Future investigations should continue to explore the effects of goal setting on a wide range of motor skills in the instructional setting to determine if the facilitative effect of participative goal setting can be generalized across various motor skills.

References

Barnett, M. L. Effects of student-led small group and teacher-pupil conference methods of goal-setting on achievement in a gross motor task. Unpublished doctoral dissertation, University of Michigan, August, 1975.

Barnett, M. L. Effects of two methods of goal setting on learning a gross motor task. *Research Quarterly*, 1977, *48*, 17–23.

Bryan, J. F., & Locke, E. A. Goal setting as a means of increasing motivation. *Journal of Applied Psychology*, 1967, *51*, 274–77.

Gaa, J. P. *Goal setting behavior, achievement in reading, and attitude toward reading associated with individual goal setting conferences* (Technical report 142). The University of Wisconsin, Research and Development Center for Cognitive Learning, 1970.

Harvey, A. L. *Goal-setting behavior in high school girls*. Unpublished doctoral dissertation, Cornell University, 1971.

Hollingsworth, B. Effects of performance goals and anxiety on learning a gross motor task. *Research Quarterly*, 1975, *46*, 162–68.

Kim, J. S., & Hamner, W. S. Effects of performance feedback and goal setting. *Journal of Applied Psychology*, 1976, *61*, 48–57.

Latham, G. P., & Baldes, J. J. Practical significance of Locke's theory of goal-setting. *Journal of Applied Psychology*, 1975, *60*, 122–24.

Latham, G. P., & Yukl, G. A. Assigned versus participative goal setting with educated and uneducated woods workers. *Journal of Applied Psychology*, 1975, *60*, 299–302.

Latham, G. P., & Yukl, G. A. Effects of assigned and participative goal setting on performance and job satisfaction. *Journal of Applied Psychology*, 1976, *61*, 166–171.

Locke, E. A. Toward a theory of task motivation and incentives. *Organizational Behavior and Human Performance*, 1968, *3*, 157–189.

Locke, E. A., & Bryan, J. A. Cognitive aspects of psychomotor performance: The effects of performance goals on level of performance. *Journal of Applied Psychology*, 1966, *50*, 286–291.

Locke, E. A., & Bryan, J. A. Performance goals as determinants of level of performance and boredom. *Journal of Applied Psychology*, 1967, *51*, 120–130.

Locke, E. A., Bryan, J. A., & Kendall, L. M. Goals and intentions as mediators of the effects of monetary incentives on behavior. *Journal of Applied Psychology*, 1968, *52*, 104–121.

Marliave, R. S. *Attitudes, self-esteem, achievement, and goal-setting behavior associated with goal setting conferences in reading skills* (Technical report 176). The University of Wisconsin, Wisconsin Research and Development Center for Cognitive Learning, 1970.

Submitted: 5 January, 1979
Accepted: 16 May, 1979

SELF-TEST FOR TASK 1-A

Effects of Goal Setting on Achievement in Archery

The Problem

_____

_____

_____

The Procedures

_____

_____

_____

_____

_____

_____

_____

The Method of Analysis

_____

_____

_____

The Major Conclusion(s)

_____

_____

_____

Basic Concepts in the Oral Directions of Group Achievement Tests

JACK A. CUMMINGS
R. BRETT NELSON
University of Georgia

Reprinted from the Journal of Educational Research, 1980, 73 (5), 259-261, by permission.

ABSTRACT The teacher's oral directions of primary group achievement tests were analyzed for the presence of Boehm's basic concepts. The *California Achievement Test, Iowa Test of Basic Skills, Metropolitan Achievement Tests,* and *Stanford Diagnostic Reading Test* were all found to include numerous basic concepts in their directions. Because first graders and, to a lesser extent, second graders have difficulty mastering basic concepts, the construct validity of subtests assessing skills other than language was questioned. Implications of the results for teacher administration of primary level tests as well as suggestions for future test construction were described.

B oehm (1) recognized the importance of basic concepts in his review of preschool and primary curriculum materials in the areas of arithmetic, reading, and science. The purpose of the review was to discover concepts or terms that met the following criteria: (a) occurred frequently, (b) were seldom explained or explained in the simplest form and then used in a more complex manner, (c) were relatively abstract. After selecting numerous basic concepts, kindergarten and first grade children were tested for their understanding of them. Those concepts that were most frequently misunderstood were included in the *Boehm Test of Basic Concepts.*

In addition to classroom instruction, basic concepts also pervade individual preschool assessment. Kaufman (6) reported that examiner's oral directions of the *Wechsler Preschool and Primary Scale of Intelligence* had fourteen basic concepts. Kaufman questioned the construct validity of performance scale subtests due to the conceptual complexity of the verbal instructions; that is, if the examinee doesn't understand basic concepts in the directions is it safe to assume he or she will correctly perceive the tasks demand?

A logical extension of Kaufman's conclusions would encompass group testing. The purpose of this study is to answer the following question: are basic concepts included in the teacher's oral directions of commonly used group achievement tests?

Method

The following primary level group achievement tests were screened for basic concepts within the teacher's oral directions: *California Achievement Tests,* 1970 edition, Level 1, Form A, Grades 1.5 - 2.0 (8); *Iowa Tests of Basic Skills* 1972 edition, Level 7, Form 5, Grades 1.7 - 1.5 (4); *Metropolitan Achievement Tests,* 1978 edition, Primer Level, Form JS, Grades K.5 - 1.4 (7); *Stanford Diagnostic Reading Test,* 1976 edition, Red Level, Grades 1.5 - 2.5 (5).

Procedure

Only teacher's directions intended to orient students to the task demands were included in the analyses. The following test item will demonstrate the analysis procedure: "Now look at *row 26,* at the *top* of the *second* column. There is a picture of a line with an arrow above it. What does the picture show? Fill in the oval under the number fact shown by the picture." The function of the first sentence is to help the student find the correct test item in the booklet. It assumes the student understands the underlined basic concepts—that is, row, top, second. The second and latter sentences would not be included in the analysis. The purpose of these sentences is to assess the child's ability to grasp the meaning of the combination of concepts.

Boehm's basic concepts were used in the analysis because of the rational and empirical criteria employed during test construction. The Boehm test items were selected by the proportion of children at the kindergarten, first, second, and third grade levels who passed each item and on the basis of the point biserial correlation of each item with the subject's total score. Based on these statistics the fifty most difficult concepts were selected to compose the *Boehm Test of Basic Concepts.*

Included in the norms are percentages of children passing each item at the kindergarten, first, and second grade levels. Data are also provided regarding socioeconomic levels. For example, in the national standardization sample, 31 percent of lower socioeconomic first graders

No other research stated.

missed the concept "second," whereas 9 percent of the middle and 8 percent of higher socioeconomic first graders misunderstood the concept. In summary, Boehm's basic concepts were chosen for the analysis because the norms document that first graders and, to a lesser extent, second graders have difficulty grasping their meaning.

Results and Discussion

All the achievement tests surveyed assumed children understood numerous basic concepts. Inspection of Table I reveals that Boehm's basic concepts are frequently used in the teacher's oral directions to subtests. The *Metropolitan Achievement Test* used the largest number of Boehm's concepts, whereas the *Iowa Test of Basic Skills* and *Stanford Diagnostic Reading Test* used the least.

The importance of basic concepts within the teacher's oral directions may be demonstrated with the following quote from the *Stanford Diagnostic Reading Test,* Test I, Auditory Vocabulary. If after the examiner explains the tast, children still don't comprehend what is expected of them, then the examiner says, "As we do the questions, we will go down one *side* of the paper and then down the *other.*" According to Boehm (2) 25 percent of the lower socioeconomic children in first grade wouldn't understand the former concept while 18 percent will fail to comprehend the latter. Consider a hypothetical classroom of thirty lower socioeconomic children. Approximately eight wouldn't understand the concept of "side" and six would be baffled by "other ." Returning to the example, it is likely that this direction will further confuse the child rather than help him to understand the demands of the task.

It is the researchers' contention that the construct validity of a subtest that purports to assess abilities other than language is questionable when basic concepts are used in the oral directions. Kaufman (6) states that when a child does not understand what is expected of him for a given task, his abilities on the task are probably not being assessed validly. Therefore, when a child does poorly on a subtest, one could question whether his ability or communication skills are deficit.

The present findings have direct implications for the classroom teacher administering group achievement tests. In order to insure that students perform in a manner consistent with their maximum potential the following guidelines should be observed: *Suggestions to students:*

1) Limit testing to groups of ten or less so that each child may be individually monitored. In this manner the teacher will know that every child is working on the correct page and test item. If the class is larger than ten it may be possible to divide the class and send half the children to a supervised play area. Another solution may be to use a classroom aid with whom the children are familiar. The aid or paraprofessional may then assist the teacher in monitoring the students for difficulties that may arise during the course of test administration. It is recommended that the person who assists the test administrator should be briefed regarding proper testing procedure prior to the administration. The test manual should always be consulted for the types of help that may be given to students.

2) The test administration should begin only after all children have correctly answered the sample questions. If a child makes an error on the sample, the teacher or aid should determine the source of the difficulty and then begin testing after the problem has been resolved.

3) If practice booklets are available they are an invaluable aid for familiarizing the student with the testing format. If after administering the sample test a teacher notes that a student hasn't answered above the level of chance, the practice test may be readministered until the directions are clear to the child. The actual test or test items should not be readministered.

4) Because basic concepts are at times pivotal words in the teacher's oral directions, it would be advisable to assess the class's understanding of these words prior to testing. If the results of the class's performance on the *Boehm Test of Basic Concepts* indicates that many children have weaknesses in certain concepts used in an upcoming group achievement test, remediation of those concepts would be beneficial. Suggestions for the instruction of basic concepts are contained in the *Boehm Resource Guide for Basic Concept Teaching,* (3).

5) A last consideration is the vision and hearing abilities of the students. Prior to test administration, all should have passed both hearing and vision screenings.

The present study also has implications for future test construction. These are:

1) Directions to subtests should be carefully worded so difficult concepts are kept to a minimum. It is also the researcher's contention that oral directions be reduced to the bare essentials. Based on personal experi-

Table 1. Boehm's Basic Concepts in the Examiner's Oral Directions of Primary Level Group Achievement Tests

California Achievement Tests	Iowa Test of Basic Skills	Metropolitan Achievement Test	Stanford Diagnostic Reading Test
begin	after	begin	beginnings
different	begin	different	below
first	below	first	next to
last	different	last	other
most	middle	left	over
next to	second	middle	second
other	through	next to	side
over	top	other	top
row		right	
second		row	
top		second	
		side	
		some	
		third	
		top	

ence, we have observed that difficulties with classroom management are most frequent during extended periods of oral directions. In other words talking, looking at a neighbor's paper, and acting up are most common when the teacher is required to read lengthy directions.

2) Sample items may be improved by having the examiner use poster-size test booklets. Rather than having the student do the first sample item, using the poster-size test, the examiner may model the required task. By having the child see the correct procedure it may reduce the possibility of failure on the sample item.

3) When the achievement test is in the developmental phase, directions should be checked for conceptual complexity. During the national tryouts the instructions may be evaluated to determine what percentage of children understand them. Perhaps an arbitrary criterion of 95 percent would be useful for insuring that a substantial percentage of children understand the directions. Thus,

the test publisher would be more assured that the task demands rather than the understanding of oral directions were being assessed.

4) Test publishers should be encouraged to continue the present trend of including practice booklets with group-administered achievement tests. As previously mentioned the practice test serves to acquaint children with the structure and demands of the actual test. In addition the well-designed sample test booklet could be used as an educational tool to teach the more difficult concepts used in directions of the actual test.

In conclusion, the teacher's oral directions for commonly used group achievement tests frequently contain basic concepts. The authors contend that the construct validity of those subtests that are intended to evaluate skills other than language are questionable. If a student performs poorly on such a task one must question whether the student actually understood the task demands.

NOTE

An earlier version of this paper was presented at the Annual Meeting of the Georgia Educational Research Association, November, 1979.

REFERENCES

1. Boehm, A.E. "The Development of Comparative Concepts in Primary School Children." Doctoral dissertation, Columbia University) Ann Arbor, Michigan: University Microfilms, 1967. No. 67-5767.
2. Boehm, A. E. *Boehm Test of Basic Concepts Manual.* New York: Psychological Corporation, 1971.
3. Boehm, A. E. *Boehm Resource Guide for Basic Concepts Teaching.* New York: Psychological Corporation, 1977.
4. Hieronymus, A. N., and Lindquist, E. F. *Teacher's Guide Iowa Tests of Basic Skills,* Grades 1.7 - 2.4. The University of Iowa, 1972.
5. Karlsen, B.: Madden, R.; and Gardener, E. F. *Stanford Diagnostic Reading Test Manual for Administering and Interpreting.* New York: Harcourt Brace Jovanvovich, Inc. 1976.
6. Kaufman, A. S. "The Importance of Basic Concepts in the Individual Assessment of Preschool Children. " *Journal of School Psychology* 16 (1978): 207- 11.
7. Prescott, G. A.; Balow, I. H.; Hogan, T. P.; and Farr, R. C. *Metropolitan Achievement Tests Teacher's Manual.* New York: The Psychological Corporation, 1978.
8. Tiegs, E. W., and Clark, W. W. *Examiner's Manual California Achievement Tests.* Monterey, California: CTB/McGraw-Hill, 1970.

SELF-TEST FOR TASK 1-A

Basic Concepts in the Oral Directions
of Group Achievement Tests

The Problem

Are basic concepts used by teachers when they
give oral directions on group

The Procedures

Used 4 basic standard test

& took the basic

The Method of Analysis

The Major Conclusion(s)

Testing Versus Review: Effects on Retention

Ronald J. Nungester and Philippe C. Duchastel
The American College

Taking a test on content that has just been studied is known to enhance later retention of the material studied, but is testing more profitable than the same amount of time spent in review? High school students studied a brief history text, then either took a test on the passage, spent equivalent time reviewing the passage, or went on to an unrelated task. A retention test given 2 weeks later indicated that the test condition resulted in better retention than either the review or the control conditions. The effect was further shown to be content specific (in contrast to effects typically produced by questions inserted in text) and independent of item format. These results favor a greater use of testing in instruction.

Administering quizzes to students in class is generally considered to fulfill two functions: to motivate students to study and to determine how well they have mastered the material that was taught. A third function, more directly related to the learning process, goes largely unrecognized: to help the student consolidate in memory what was learned. It is this third function of testing with which the present research is concerned.

This consolidation function of testing was demonstrated relatively early in instructional psychology (Jones, 1923–1924) and replicated on numerous occasions (e.g., Laporte & Voss, 1975). This consolidation effect is described as follows: taking a test immediately after learning will lead to better retention of the material at a later date, as evidenced on a delayed retention test, even when no corrective feedback is provided and when no further study of the material has taken place.

Recent research (Duchastel, 1981; Nungester & Duchastel, Note 1) has examined how this consolidation effect (known simply as a testing effect on retention) was influenced by the type of test employed. Two test formats were considered: short-answer tests and multiple-choice tests. This research initially indicated an advantage for short-answer tests but later demonstrated that multiple-choice tests can be just as potent for enhancing retention. Thus, at the moment, there is no strong basis for concluding that one type of test has the advantage over the other for consolidating learning. Our previous research (Nungester & Duchastel, Note 1) has also shown that the consolidation effect is independent of the simple test practice effect derived from repeated testing with the same type of test. That is, a testing effect can also be demonstrated on a retention test cast in a different format (e.g., on a multiple-choice retention test when the initial test was a short-answer one).

Of practical concern to teachers is the question of whether the time devoted to testing might be spent as profitably by allowing students to study the material more. Is spending some portion of a teaching session in testing really more valuable than spending that same time in further study? The present experiment principally addressed this applied question.

From a learning process point of view, this experiment examined the possibility that observed testing effects are not due to testing itself but result from the fact that experimental groups spend more total time on a topic (learning time and testing time) than do the control groups typically employed (who spend the same amount of time on the learning task, but then go on to some other

We wish to acknowledge the assistance of the Haverford Township School District, Delaware County, Pennsylvania, in the conduct of this study, especially the teachers who assisted directly: Mr. Bush, Mrs. McGarvey, Miss Harrison, Mr. Long, and their principal, Mr. Drukin.

Requests for reprints should be sent to Ronald J. Nungester, The American College, 270 Bryn Mawr Ave., Bryn Mawr, Pennsylvania 19010.

task used as a filler task, such as completing a study habits inventory or the like). This argument is called the total-time hypothesis and has been invoked in the connex area of research on adjunct aids as a competing explanation for the results obtained in many experimental situations such as these (Faw & Waller, 1976). The total-time hypothesis thus vies with the consolidation hypothesis as an explanation for the effects of testing on later retention. The design of the present study allowed these two hypotheses to confront one another and thus offered a serious test of the consolidation hypothesis.

Three groups of students studied a brief history text, after which the first group was tested on the passage, the second group was allowed further study of the text for an equivalent amount of time, and the third group was directed to an unrelated (filler) task. A retention test on the passage was administered to all students 2 weeks later. It was expected that performance on this retention test would be strongest for the group initially tested following learning, next strongest for the group allowed further study, and weakest for the filler task group.

A further refinement in the design (described in the next section) permitted a replication of our previous findings with respect to test format, as well as an examination of how the testing of some content might affect the later retention of other, initially untested, content. The primary aim of the experiment, however, was to contrast testing with further studying, as indicated above.

Method

Subjects

The students participating in the experiment were 97 senior students from a middle-class suburban high school. They participated in the experiment as part of their regular school program. The students were randomly assigned to the three conditions in the study.

Materials

The learning passage employed in this study was the same one that was employed in the previous two studies by the authors. It consisted of a 1,700-word passage entitled "The Victorian Era," which contained 12 topical paragraphs describing events in British history (1837–1901 period). The passage had been adapted from other sources by one of the present authors so that it could be easily understood by high school students. The passage is more fully described by Duchastel (1981).

Design and Procedure

The experiment involved two experimental groups and one control group. The first group, the test group, studied the passage for 15 minutes, then took an immediate test on its contents (initial test). No feedback was provided. The second group studied the passage for 15 minutes, then spent additional time reviewing the passage. This group was labeled the review group. The control group studied the passage for 15 minutes, then completed a learning process questionnaire that served as a filler task. This filler task simply served to occupy the students in this group while the other students were either completing the initial test or reviewing the passage. The time allocated for either treatment (test or review) or for the filler task was 5 minutes.

Two weeks later, all students were administered a retention test on the contents of the materials.

The history passage used in the experiment was collected after the students had initially studied it and was therefore not available to the students during the interval between the two experimental sessions. Their teachers were furthermore asked not to discuss this part of history with them until after the retention test. A questionnaire administered to the students at the conclusion of the experiment inquired about any discussion of the text with friends during the 2-week interval.

The teachers were aware of an eventual retention test, but the students themselves were not told of such a test. To provide some apparent conclusion to the experiment at the end of the first session, the students were administered a brief elaborative processing inventory, developed by Schmeck, Ribich, and Ramanaiah (1977). Bringing closure to the initial session in this way was especially important for the review and control groups, since they were not tested on the content of the passage during this session.

Tests

The initial test, which was administered to the students in the test group only, contained 12 questions that selectively sampled the contents of the passage. Every odd-numbered question was in a multiple-choice format (e.g., "What nationality was Prince Albert? a) German; b) Russian; c) Hungarian."); and every even-numbered question was in a short-answer format (e.g., "In which part of the world was the Crimean War? _____"). Each of the 12 questions corresponded to one of the 12 topics in the passage.

The retention test, which was administered 2 weeks later to all students in the study, contained 24 questions (two questions per topic). For the test group, half of these questions were old questions that required recall or recognition of the same information as requested on the initial test. The other half of the questions were new questions for this group. For the review and control groups, all questions on the retention test were in fact new questions, since neither of these groups were tested in the initial session.

The questions the test group had seen on the initial test (old questions) were transformed into the alternate question format on the retention test. Thus, multiple-choice questions on the initial test became short-answer questions on the retention test, and vice versa. To the illustrative questions presented above corresponded the following questions: "What nationality was Prince Albert? _____" and "In which part of the world was the Crimean War? a) the Near East; b) North-Africa; c) India." Reversal of item format in this way enabled us to replicate some of the conditions found in our previous study (Nungester & Duchastel, Note 1).

As can be seen from the illustrative questions above, all questions were at the information level of knowledge.

Results

The retention test scores are presented in Table 1. With respect to the total test scores, the pattern of results indicated that the test group performed best of all, followed by the review group and then the control group. An analysis of variance performed on these scores revealed a significant difference, $F(2, 94) = 4.0$, $p < .05$, but further planned contrasts between each pair of groups revealed that only the difference between the test group and the control group was statistically significant, $p < .05$. The sample difference between the test group and the review group was not significant. These results have implications for the total-time hypothesis and are discussed in the next section.

In the first part of Table 1, the total test scores are partitioned according to whether

Table 1
Means and Standard Deviations of Scores on the Retention Test (Subsets of Items and Total Test)

Group	Subset A		Subset B		Total	
	M	SD	M	SD	M	SD
Test[a] (n = 31)	7.7	2.3	4.7	2.7	12.4	4.5
Review (n = 34)	5.7	1.8	5.3	2.0	11.0	3.1
Control (n = 32)	5.0	2.1	4.6	2.5	9.7	3.9

Note. The test contained 24 items.
[a] For this group only, Subset A represents items repeated from the initial test; Subset B represents new items.

Table 2
Means and Standard Deviations of the Retention Test Scores Partitioned According to Question Format (Total Test and Old Items Only)

Group	Total test				Old items only			
	MC		SA		MC		SA	
	M	SD	M	SD	M	SD	M	SD
Test	7.1	2.3	5.3	2.6	4.3	1.3	3.5	1.3
Review	6.7	1.6	4.3	2.0	3.4	.9	2.4	1.2
Control	6.0	2.2	3.7	2.5	3.2	1.3	1.8	1.3

Note. MC = multiple-choice questions; SA = short-answer questions.

the questions represent new or old items in terms of the prior experience of the test group. For the other two groups, all questions were new ones and the partition only serves to provide baselines with which to compare the two subsets of items identified in the case of the test group.

Analyses of variance were performed on both subsets of items and revealed that a significant difference existed in the case of old items but not in the case of new items, $F(2, 94) = 14.6$, $p < .001$, and $F(2, 94) < 1$, respectively. Planned contrasts within the subset of old items revealed that the test group differed significantly from both the review and control groups ($p < .001$, in each case). Thus, the benefits of testing were limited to old items and did not extend to new ones.

Another way of partitioning the total test scores is in terms of the format of the questions: multiple-choice or short-answer. The partitioned scores are presented in Table 2. Analyses of variance on each set of questions for the total test revealed that a significant difference existed only in the case of the short-answer questions, $F(2, 94) = 3.9$, $p < .05$. However, when only old items were considered (these being the only items that revealed a testing effect in the previous analysis), the partition revealed that a significant difference existed in both the case of short-answer questions and of multiple-choice questions, $Fs(2, 94) = 13.7$ and 7.3, $p < .001$ and $p < .05$, respectively. Thus, testing effects were not limited by item format.

Finally, the brief questionnaire administered to the students at the end of the study indicated that a number of students thought about the text contents or discussed them among themselves in the intersession interval. The proportion of students who did so ranged from 60% (test and control groups) to 70% (review group). To examine how this intersession activity might have influenced the retention results, the data were re-analyzed with the students partitioned into those who did discuss the text contents and those who did not. The results of these analyses did not differ from those reported above. Furthermore, the correlation between the initial test and the retention test calculated in the case of the test group was .78. Thus, although intersession activity may have slightly increased overall retention performance, it did not do so differentially between the groups.

Discussion

The principal aim of this study was to examine a practical issue concerning the testing effect: Should students spend some portion of learning time on testing or simply devote that time to study or continued review? The results of the study indicate that testing is indeed more profitable for retention.

Although review itself is profitable, as indicated by a sample increase of 10% in retention over control group performance (total test scores), testing is even more profitable (resulting in a sample increase of 25% over control group performance). Testing thus appears to have the advantage.

This decision-oriented conclusion may seem to be at odds with the fact that the contrast between testing and review on total test performance was not statistically significant. This, however, was true only for total test performance. When subsets of the test questions were examined in terms of the old versus new items for the test group, the results were different: The groups do not differ on new items, but the test group is superior to both other groups on old items. It is this particular result that leads us to conclude that testing has a definite advantage over review, as explained below.

The design of the study called for initial testing with only half of the items that constituted the retention test. It is on these items that students in the test group showed an advantage over review students on the retention test. Had the initial test comprised all of the items on the retention test, it is most likely that this advantage would have been evident in total test performance. We therefore feel that it is warranted at this time, given the difference between groups on old items, to conclude that testing is indeed more advantageous for retention than is review.

This same interpretation also extends to the more theoretical issue concerning the total-time hypothesis. The previous research on testing had shown that testing can enhance retention, but no account had been taken of the additional time required for testing. The present experiment demonstrated that testing remains beneficial even when such testing replaces actual study (review) time. The total-time hypothesis therefore does not limit the validity of the testing effect, nor does it limit the applicability of the testing principle to actual practices in school settings.

It remains possible of course that more difficult or complex texts requiring greater comprehension skills would profit more from additional study than did the factually oriented text used in this study. Until the generalizability of the present results are further examined, conclusions should be restricted to the testing of factual materials.

Whereas the focus of this experiment was the practical issue discussed above, the design was additionally motivated by a desire to partially replicate our previous findings with respect to the retention of content initially untested (Duchastel, 1981) and with respect to test format (Nungester & Duchastel, Note 1).

Our design decision to employ a retention test that comprised both items seen before by the test group (old items) and items not previously seen (new items) was aimed at determining whether testing has a specific or a general effect in terms of consolidation. That is, are only contents covered by the initial test in fact consolidated, or do other contents in the passage also share in this process of consolidation, even though they are not represented on the initial test?

In the mathemagenics literature, both specific and general processes have been demonstrated to result from inserted post questions (McGaw & Grotelueschen, 1972; Rickards, 1979). In the literature dealing with the testing effect however, only a specific process has been demonstrated: Both Laporte and Voss (1975) and Duchastel (1981) have found that the testing of specific content enhances retention of that content, but does not enhance the retention of other, initially untested, content. The present findings further support this conclusion: Old items on the retention test were better answered by the test group when compared with the other two groups, but not new items. Consolidation would thus appear to be limited to the contents of the passage that are tested. This conclusion points to a major area of divergence between the mathemagenics literature and the testing effect literature.

A second design decision in this study was to employ both short-answer and multiple-choice questions on the initial test and to reverse the test format of these items on the retention test. This arrangement does not permit a true experimental test of the item format issue (for lack of a control condition for which item format would not be reversed), but it does permit a partial replication of our previous finding that the testing effect is not fully confounded with a test practice effect (Nungester & Duchastel, Note 1). This replication was positive: A testing effect was obtained with our items even though test format was reversed. We are therefore more confident in our previous conclusion that the testing effect does indeed involve consolidation and is not merely an artifact of a repeated test format.

The replication also confirmed our earlier result that testing effects are not greatly influenced by initial item format; indeed, testing effects are as readily obtained with multiple-choice items as with short-answer ones.

Practical Considerations

The previous research on testing had established that testing can be a potent way of enhancing retention. The present study demonstrated that testing is superior to review for that purpose; thus, although testing takes time away from study, that time is well spent.

It should be noted that the present study involved unguided review in the form of additional study time. Directed review activities that structure the review, whether encouraged by written instructions following the text or led by a teacher, would possibly attenuate the advantage of testing. Directed review might in fact serve in this respect the consolidation function offered by testing.

As indicated in our introduction, educators are apt to value testing (in the form of quizzes) for motivational and diagnostic purposes. The research on the testing effect adds a further dimension to the use of quizzes. As such, it should encourage educators to make greater use of testing in instruction.

Reference Note

1. Nungester, R. J., & Duchastel, P. C. *Testing effects measured with alternate test forms.* Paper presented at the meeting of the American Educational Research Association, Los Angeles, 1981.

References

Duchastel, P. Retention of prose following testing with different types of test. *Contemporary Educational Psychology*, 1981, *6*, 217–226.

Faw, H. W., & Waller, T. G. Mathemagenic behaviors and efficiency in learning from prose. *Review of Educational Research*, 1976, *46*, 691–720.

Jones, H. E. The effects of examination on the performance of learning. *Archives of Psychology*, 1923–1924, *10*, 1–70.

Laporte, R., & Voss, J. Retention of prose materials as a function of postacquisition testing. *Journal of Educational Psychology*, 1975, *67*, 259–266.

McGaw, B., & Grotelueschen, A. Direction of the effect of questions in prose material. *Journal of Educational Psychology*, 1972, *63*, 580–588.

Rickards, J. Adjunct postquestions in text: A critical review of methods and processes. *Review of Educational Research*, 1979, *49*, 181–196.

Schmeck, R., Ribich, F., & Ramanaiah, N. Development of a self-report inventory for assessing individual differences in learning processes. *Applied Psychological Measurement*, 1977, *1*, 413–431.

Received January 27, 1981 ■

SELF-TEST FOR TASK 1-A

Testing Versus Review: Effects on Retention

The Problem

Whether the time spent testing might be spent as profitably by allowing students to study the material more.

The Procedures

97 sr. students from a middle class suburban H.S. Stud. randomly assigned selected to the 3 conditions in the study. The used 1700 word passage "the Victorian Era" - British history (1837- 1901).

1st group - test group: study 15 mins then took test - no feedback
2nd group - 15 mins study, spent add'l time reviewing   (review group)
3rd group - 15 mins study then compl. a learning process questionaire.

2 wks later all student were given a retention test

Ques. was given after the test to see if any discussion about the history had taken place

The Method of Analysis

Analyses of the variance were performed on test results.

The Major Conclusion(s)

Testing is the most profitable for retention.

Task 1-B

> Given reprints of three research studies, classify each
> as historical, descriptive, correlational, causal-com-
> parative, or experimental research and list the charac-
> teristics of each study which support the classification
> chosen.

Part One includes a number of examples for each of the methods of research. Reread them and see if you can come up with some examples of your
own. After you have generated some examples, ask yourself the questions
presented within the section of Part One entitled Guidelines for Classifica-
tion. If the answers to those questions suggest that each example does indeed represent the method of research you intended it to represent, you are
in business (that means you are probably ready for Task 1-B). As a self-test,
classify by method the preceding research reports; use the form which follows.
If all your choices and reasons agree with the Suggested Responses, you are
definitely ready for Task 1-B. If you miss one, make sure you understand why
you were in error. If you miss several, and especially if you do not understand why, see your instructor.

SELF-TEST FOR TASK 1-B

Meaning as a Factor in Predicting Spelling Difficulty

Method: _____

Reasons: _____

_____

_____

_____

_____

The Effect of Male Teachers on the Academic
Achievement of Father-Absent Sixth Grade Boys

Method: _____

Reasons: _____

_____

_____

_____

_____

Prestigious Psycho-Educational Research Published
From 1910 to 1974: Types of Explanations,
Focus, Authorship, and Other Concerns

Method: _____

Reasons: _____

_____

_____

_____

_____

Effects of Goal Setting on Achievement in Archery

Method: _____

Reasons: _____

_____

_____

_____

_____

Basic Concepts in the Oral Directions
of Group Achievement Tests

Method: _____

Reasons: _____

_____

_____

_____

_____

Testing Versus Review: Effects on Retention

Method: _____

Reasons:_____

_____

_____

_____

_____

PART TWO

RESEARCH PROBLEMS

EXERCISES

EXERCISE II - 1

In each item below, you are given a brief description of subjects (X), an independent variable (Y), and a dependent variable (Z). For each X, Y, and Z, write a directional research hypothesis.
(Statement in some direction)

1. X = hyperactive primary-level children
   Y = type of therapy (diet versus drug)
   Z = on-task behavior

Hyperactive primary-level children on the diet therapy show greater improvement on-task behavior than children on drug therapy.

2. X = college-level introductory psychology students
   Y = type of testing (short-answer versus multiple-choice)
   Z = retention of psychological concepts and principles

indep: type of test
dep: retention

College-level intr. psych. students who take short ans. testing have better retention than students who take mult-choice tests.

3. X = public school students
   Y = high school graduation
   Z = income at age 25

Public school students who grad. have higher income than P.S. students who do not grad.

4. X = junior high school students
   Y = verbal reinforcement (positive versus negative)
   Z = absenteeism

Junior high school students who rec. positive verbal reinforcement have less absenteeism than those J.R.H.S. std. who rec. neg. verbal reinforcement

36

5. X = upper elementary students
   Y = type of drill and practice (computer assisted versus teacher directed)
   Z - computational skill

Upper elem. students who rec. computer assisted type of drill + practice have better computational skill than upper elem. school students who rec. teacher directed drill & practice.

EXERCISE II - 2

there is no statiscally significant difference between X & Y.

For each X,Y and Z in Exercise II-1, write a null hypothesis.

1. On task behavior in hyperactive primary-level children does not sign. vary whether they rec. diet or drug therapy.

2. there is no significant difference between the retention of psychological concepts + principles for college-level introductory psychology students whose rec. short-ans. vs multiple choice type of testing.

3. there is no sign. diff. in the income of P.S. student who graduate and those who don't graduate.

4.

5. _____

_____

_____

_____

PART TWO

RESEARCH PROBLEMS

TASK 2

> Write an introduction for a research plan. This will in-
> clude a statement of the specific problem to be investi-
> gated in the study, a statement concerning the signifi-
> cance of the problem, a review of related literature, and
> a testable hypothesis. Include definitions of terms
> where appropriate.

Since in succeeding Parts you will be performing Tasks as they relate to
your problem, you should give careful thought to the selection of a problem.
Also, since the research competencies required for the conducting of an experimental study include many of the competencies required for conduction of
studies representing the other methods of research, and more, it is to your
advantage to select a problem which can be investigated experimentally; you
will acquire experience with a wider range of competencies and should be able
to generalize many of those competencies as they apply to the other methods
of research.

Task 2 involves the writing of an introduction to a research plan which
follows the guidelines described in Part Two. Following this discussion,
five examples are presented which illustrate the format and content of such
an introduction. These examples, with few modifications, represent Tasks
submitted by former students in an introductory research course. Examples
from published research could have been used, but these examples more accurately reflect the performance which is expected of you at your current level
of research expertise.

The Effectiveness of the Use of Hand-Held Calculators in Tenth Grade General Math Classes[1]

Introduction

The advent of statewide competency tests of basic skills in Mathematics (and English) for all juniors in the high schools of North Carolina underlines the urgency for the most modern and effective methods of instruction. The competency tests are being instigated due, in part, to the fact that many students have graduated in the past without the minimum level of computational and problem solving ability deemed necessary for successful citizenship in our time. Along with the testing program, the State Department of Public Instruction has committed an enormous amount of money for remedial instructional personnel and meterials. Students who fail the mathematics portion of the test will be placed in the remedial class and have the opportunity to retake it in their senior year.

At the same time, a controversy exists among mathematics educators concerning the value of the use of hand-held calculators in the classroom as an aid to teaching computational skills. With the cost of calculators decreasing due to advanced technologies and competition between manufacturers, it is becoming more and more realistic for school systems and families to purchase them. The controversy is not over the cost of calculators, however, but rather, their use in the classroom. Most educators agree that there is a place for pencil and paper algorithms within the framework of computational instruction. In light of the competency tests and calculator technology, many educators are now debating the issue of where the use of the calculator fits into the curriculum.

Statement of the Problem

The problem to be investigated in this study is the effectiveness of the use of hand-held calculators in tenth grade general mathematics classes.

Review of Related Literature

Opinions concerning the worth of calculator use in the classroom range from considering their use as a great shot in the arm to virtual condemnation. Proponents cite a variety of reasons for inclusion of calculators into the curriculum. One of the primary goals of a school mathematics program is student achievement in computational skills (Trafton & Suydam, 1975). The use of mathematics in real-life situations dictates this goal. Consequently, the use of calculators as a reinforcer of basic skills seems to be a reasonable technique. In fact, many studies have been done using such a method. In addition to the reinforcement aspects of calculators, they are considered by many to be a motivational tool (Caravella, 1977).

Professional organizations have taken a varied, although generally positive, position on calculator usage. According to the recommendation of the National Advisory Committee on Mathematics Education, "by ninth grade a calculator should be available to all students at all times" (Caravella, 1977). Such a liberal approach to the problem is not found to be shared by

---

[1] Based on a paper by R.P. Catapano, North Carolina State University, Raleigh, 1978.

many authors, however. A more likely position is one taken by the Board of Directors of the National Council of Teachers of Mathematics: "With the decrease in cost of the minicalculator, its accessibility to students at all levels is increasing rapidly. Mathematics teachers should recognize the potential contribution of this calculator as a valuable instructional aid. In the classroom, the minicalculator should be used in imaginative ways to reinforce the learner as he becomes proficient in mathematics" (Shumway, 1976).

   Another arguement for the use of calculators suggests that just as paper and pencil are tools of calculation and algorithms are methods of calculation, so are calculators the tools of calculation. Take away the tools from any student and he cannot calculate. Why not use the calculators and eliminate the mechanical (algorithmic) nature of computation? (Hopkins, 1977)

   Opponents of the use of calculators typically believe that students need to know why a certain solution is the answer and that such a question cannot be resolved by a person dependent on a calculator. In short, they feel that calculators "lead to a decay of the understanding of arithmetic in those who already understand basic skills and prevent the learning by others" (Hopkins, 1977). More specifically, negative side effects often cited include: decrease in student motivation for learning basic skills (proponents feel otherwise), inappropriateness for slow learners, reduction of students' ability to detect errors, and the "old standby" question -- what if the batteries lose their charge? (Shumway, 1976)

   The vast majority of educators seem to take a position between these extremes. For this reason, it is necessary for school districts to develop policies on calculator usage. The policy should address questions such as: Are the calculators to be used as the tool for computation or as a check of calculations done by hand?...At what grade should their use be introduced?... Should their use be restricted to mathematics classes only? (Munson, 1977)

   Although it seems likely that the controversy could be settled through experimental research, such a situation does not exist. Studies have been done with low achieving high school students (Cech, 1972), junior high students with learning and behavioral problems (Advani, 1972), middle school remedial math students (Aldridge, 1977), elementary school students (Schnur & Lang, 1976), and virtually every other age and ability level conceivable. Results vary as much as the subjects of the studies. Some studies generate data supporting the conclusion that experimental groups show significantly greater computational ability than noncalculator control groups (Schnur & Lang, 1976; Jones, 1976; Aldridge, 1977). Others show little or no significant statistical difference between the two groups (Mastbaum, 1969; Cech, 1972). One researcher who found that there was no significant difference theorized that it may have been due to that fact that the study was done in a very short period of time and further stated that the use of the calculator as a means of improving computational skills through reinforcement will only be effective when used for an entire school year (Cech, 1972).

Statement of the Hypothesis

   The experimental research evidence related to the effectiveness of calculators with respect to level of computational skill is inconclusive. Some studies have found no significant difference between the computational skills of calculator and non-calculator groups. Others have found a significant difference in favor of calculator groups. Typically, however, such studies have been conducted over a relatively short period of time, and it had been suggested that the effectiveness of calculators can only be demonstrated after a prolonged period of instruction such as a school year. Therefore, it is hypothesized that tenth grade general mathematics students who are taught with hand-held calculators for an eight-month period show greater achievement on tests of computational skills (taken without the use of a calculator) than their peers who are taught without calculators.

References

Advani, K. The effect of the use of desk calculators on achievement and attitude of children with learning and behavior problems. Toronto: Conference of the Ontario Educational Research Council, 1972 (ERIC ED 077 160).

Aldridge, W.S. Effects of electronic calculators on achievement of middle school remedial mathematics students (University of Georgia, 1976). Dissertations Abstracts International, 1977, 37 4078A. (University Microfilms No. 76-29, 502, 135).

Caravella, J.R. Minicalculators in the classroom. Washington, D.C.: National Education Association, 1977 (ERIC ED 134 474).

Cech, J.P. Effect of the use of desk calculators on attitude and achievement with low achieving ninth graders. Mathematics Teacher, 1972, 65, 183-186.

Hopkins, E.E. Using Hand Calculators in School, Education Digest, 1977, 42, 44-45.

Jones, E.W. The effect of the hand-held calculator on mathematics achievement, attitude, and self-concept of sixth grade students (Virginia Polytechnic Institute and State University, 1976). Dissertations Abstracts International, 1976, 37, 1387A. (University Microfilms No. 76-19, 885, 107).

Mastbaum, S. A study of the relative effectiveness of electric calculators on computational skills kits in the teaching of mathematics (University of Minnesota, 1969). Dissertations Abstracts International, 1969, 30, 2422A. (University microfilms no. 69-20, 036, 302).

Munson, H.R. Your district needs a policy on pocket calculators! Arithmetic Teacher, 1977, 25, 46.

Schnur, J.O. & Lang, J.W. Just pushing buttons or learning?--a case for minicalculators. Arithmetic Teacher, 1976, 23, 559-562.

Shumway, R.J. Hand Calculators: where do you stand? Arithmetic Teacher, 1976, 23, 569-572.

Trafton, P.R. & Suydam, M.N. Computational Skills: A point of view. Arithmetic Teacher, 1975, 22, 529-537.

Behavior Modification as an Alternative

To Amphetamine Therapy in Treating

Hyperkinesis in Children[2]

Introduction

In recent years, there has been considerable public concern and controversy over the use of amphetamines in treating hyperkinesis in children. It has been estimated that as many as 300,000 school children are now taking these drugs despite a lack of follow-up studies on the medication's long-range effects (Grinspoon & Singer, 1973; Time, 1973). Diagnosis presents another problem, for even among experts there is no consensus as to the nature of, or means for diagnosing, what is generally referred to as the hyperkinetic impulse disorder (Grinspoon & Singer, 1973). Most definitions, however, do agree on the major symptoms as: increased purpose-less activity, impaired attention span, lack of coordination, impulsivity, and poor powers of concentration, usually leading to disturbed behavior at home and at school (HEW, 1971). Estimates as to the prevalence of this disorder differ according to the source. HEW estimates a 3% incidence, while psychiatrists estimate from 4 to 10%, and some educators estimate it as high as 15 to 20% (Grinspoon & Singer, 1973).

It has been charged that many children are given amphetamines solely on the recommendations of school authorities, and that it is sometimes far too easy for teachers to mistake the normal restlessness of childhood for hyperkinesis (Time, 1973). More importantly, several investigators have found evidence of side-effects with amphetamine treatment, including addiction, insomnia, weight loss, and headaches (Ladd, 1971; Bosco, 1972). Others have asserted that the real danger is not side-effects, but that drug therapy prevents the child from learning the necessary skills of insight and self-control (Time, 1973).

In 1971, the U. S. Department of Health, Education, and Welfare called a conference of 15 specialists to review research and make recommendations on amphetamine treatment. In its report, the committee emphasized the lack of adequate longitudinal studies, and cautioned that investigation should be made into alternative treatments, including the modification of behavior by a system of positive reinforcement (HEW, 1971). Grinspoon & Singer (1973) also see behavior modification as an emerging alternative to drug therapy, stating that it teaches the child self-control and has a generalizing effect to other situations. In short, various researchers have investigated alternatives to drug therapy, with behavior modification receiving the focus of attention as being safer, and perhaps even more effective in the long run (Strong, 1974).

---

[2]Based on a paper by D. H. Hunt, Florida International University, Miami, 1974.

Statement of the Problem

This study attempted to determine the comparative effectiveness of behavior modification techniques versus amphetamine therapy in reducing the symptoms of hyperkinesis in children in a classroom setting.

For purposes of definition, the techniques of behavior modification may be classified as (1) positive reinforcement, where something positive is given when acceptable behavior occurs, (2) negative reinforcement, where unacceptable behavior is followed by a negative consequence, such as isolation, and (3) techniques using both, where desirable behaviors are encouraged by positive reinforcement while undesirable ones are discouraged by negative reinforcement (Woody, 1969).

Review of the Literature

Behavior modification procedures with respect to deviant behaviors have been subjected to numerous experimental and clinical investigations. It has been demonstrated that token reinforcement is more effective than medication in increasing adaptive behavior in retarded women (Strong, 1974). A significant decrease in hyperactive behavior among disturbed children after behavior modification therapy was reported, with carry-over into their regular school environment (Grinspoon & Singer, 1973). In a two-year experiment with a boy diagnosed as autistic, Strong (1974) demonstrated that positive reinforcement was significantly more effective than medication in reducing facial grimacing.

Besides clinical experiments, behavior modification has also been studied in school settings. Behavior modification techniques have been shown to be effective in reducing the inappropriate classroom behaviors of a ten-year-old hyperactive brain-injured boy (Woody, 1969). Another study attempted to test the effects of behavior modification in increasing task production in 24 boys rated as hyperactive by teachers (Nixon, 1969). The subjects were randomly assigned to four treatment groups, consisting of various reinforcement techniques and control. No statistically significant changes were found, although it was noted that certain children in each group made marked changes for the better. Possible sources of error, however, could have been too few treatment sessions (8), treatment groups not large enough (6 each), rater bias, since no instruments were used for evaluation, and the Hawthorne effect, since the subjects knew they were participating in a study. Finally, an interesting study by Ellis (1974) found that amphetamines had little effect on hyperactive behavior in a play setting, although it clearly affected behavior in the classroom. In conclusion, Ellis suggests that certain environmental factors might have a more potent influence on hyperactive behavior than medication. If behavior modification can be shown to be one of these factors, then perhaps an effective and safe alternative to amphetamine treatment will result.

44

In view of the above studies showing that the widespread use of amphetamines in treating hyperkinesis may be a dangerous practice, and reports showing behavior modification to be successful in treating a variety of behavioral disturbances, including hyperactivity, it was hypothesized that behavior modification techniques will be as effective as amphetamines in reducing the hyperactivity of children in a classroom setting.

References

Bosco, J. The use of ritalin for treatment of minimal brain dysfunction and hyperkinesis in children, 1972 (ERIC, ED 076 540).

Burleigh, A. Development of a scale that separates hyperkinetic and normal children and demonstrates drug effect. Paper presented at the Annual Meeting of the American Educational Research Association, New York, 1971 (ERIC, ED 048 374).

Ellis, M. J. Methylphenidate and the activity of hyperactives in the informal setting. Child Development, 1974, 45, 217-220.

Grinspoon, L., & Singer, S. Amphetamines in the treatment of hyperkinetic children. Harvard Educational Review, 1973, 43, 515-555.

Health, Education and Welfare (HEW), U. S. Department of. Report of the conference on the use of stimulant drugs in the treatment of behaviorally disturbed young school children. Washington, D.C.: Author, 1971 (ERIC, ED 051 612).

Ladd, E. G. Pills for classroom peace? Education Digest, 1971, 36, 1-4.

Nixon, S. B. Increasing the frequency of attending responses in hyperactive distractible youngsters by use of operant and modeling procedures (Doctoral dissertation, Stanford University, 1965). Dissertation Abstracts, 1966, 26, 6517. (University Microfilms No. 66-025, 97).

Time, 1973, 101, 65.

Woody, R. Behavioral Problem Children in the Schools. New York: Appleton-Century-Crofts, 1969.

The Effectiveness of the Use of Preceptors
In the Orientation of New Graduate Nurses[3]

Introduction

Before World War II, the typical nurse was trained (as opposed to educa-
ed) for three years in a hospital-based program. Upon graduation nurses
usually remained with the hospitals in which they had been trained until re-
location or marriage changed their status. There was no need for orientation
programs since the nurses were well versed in the specific policies and procedures of "their" hospitals. World War II created a shortage of nurses in
the United States and in an effort to supply more nurses for the military
nursing training was accelerated and enrollments were increased. Congress
passed the Bolton Act creating the Student War Nursing Reserve, better known
as the Cadet Nurse Corps. This Act required that nursing programs be short-
ened to two and one-half years in length and that supervised experience obtained in the military hospitals be of six months or less in duration (Rines,
1977). The Bolton Act was the forerunner of the associate degree in nursing
(ADN) program. With the inception of ADN programs in 1952 and a continual
gradual rise in baccalaureate programs, a new era was born. The college or
university campus became the "home base" for the nursing student.

This change from an apprenticeship-inservice orientation to a preservice
emphasis has been cited as a major factor in the profession leading to dissatisfaction (Cowden, 1977). As graduates of these academic programs appeared
in the market place, shortcomings in nursing programs were identified by employing agencies. No longer could an orientation to the physical plant, a
review of pertinent policies and procedures, and an introduction to the head
nurse suffice for the newcomer. Nursing service administrators were, and
still are, exceedingly vocal in expressing dissatisfaction with the clinical
experiences of graduates, ADN graduates in particular. Typically, the clinical laboratory hours in most ADN programs are one-half to one day per week
for first year students and one to two days per week for second year students
(Martin & McAdory, 1977). Research conducted by Ciatiello (1974) identified
some of the deficiencies associated with insufficient clinical experience,
such as the inability to organize and prioritize. An inventory of nursing
skills administered at the time of employment found many nonexistent or
checked in the "seen only" or "never done" column. Reality shock was observed
among graduate nurses. The nurse was educationally prepared as a beginning
practioner, but was being asked to perform as an experienced professional.

Clearly the skills and abilities expected by nursing administration are
different than those produced by nursing education. There is a need to
bridge this gap with a new approach to orientation for the new graduate. One
strategy which has been suggested involves the utilization of preceptors.

Statement of the Problem

The purpose of this study was to investigate the effectiveness of using
a preceptor in the orientation of new graduate nurses. A graduate nurse was

---

[3]Based on a paper by P.J. Ballou, Florida International University,
Miami, 1979.

defined as a graduate of a nursing program within the past six months, who may or may not have taken the state board examination for licensure as a professional nurse. A preceptor was defined as a registered professional nurse specifically chosen to act as a mentor and resource for the new graduate.

Review of Related Literature

Insufficient clinical experience on the part of many new graduate nurses has made orientation at the employing hospital a critically important activity. The need for more effective orientation has been expressed repeatedly by hospital administrators. Orientation for graduate nurses has also become a matter of financial concern for many consumers as well as hospital administrators. If the educational program is financed by public funds then the client contributes as a taxpayer and pays again in increased hospital costs because of a substantial investment in the education of the new nurse (Cantor, 1974). Costs associated with orientation of new nurses are substantial. In 1974 McClosky reported that the turnover rate for new graduates was 61% and the replacement cost to hospitals was estimated to be $20,000,000. Estimates as high as $1,500 per graduate were attributed to indirect orientation costs. In the absence of significant changes in orientation strategies, similar cost estimates for the 1980's would of course be considerably larger.

The high turnover rate for new nurses suggests that not only are hospital administrators dissatisfied with the experiences of new graduates, but also that new graduates are dissatisfied with their new jobs. Thus, the key to increasing the effectiveness of orientation periods would seem to be to increase the job satisfaction of new graduate nurses while at the same time providing them with clinical experiences needed to improve their performance. An effective orientation strategy would therefore be one which results in satisfied administrators, satisfied employees and, consequently, reduced costs. The literature suggests a number of factors which are related to job satisfaction in the nursing profession.

Everly and Falcione (1976) identified four significant variables: interpersonal relationships, intrinsic work rewards, extrinsic work rewards and administrative policies. Herzberg (1966) proposed that factors leading to satisfaction (work itself, achievement, recognition, responsibility and advancement) describe intrinsic or motivational forces and that factors leading to dissatisfaction (administrative and company policies, supervision, interpersonal relationships, working conditions, salary, status and security) are extrinsic in nature and describe the environment in which the job is done. The organization is different but the identified factors are similar in both lists. Interpersonal relationships appear to be an important aspect of job satisfaction. Head nurse leadership behavior, for example, can lead to feelings of job tension, feelings of role conflict and ambiguity, work overload and inadequate performance feedback for the nurse (Sheridan & Vredenburgh, 1978). For new graduare nurses, achievement (successful completion of tasks) and recognition (acts of praise and notice) have been identified as important sources of job satisfaction (Cronin-Stubbs, 1977). Again, human relations in general, and the behavior of superiors, emerge as important aspects of job satisfaction.

The first job is crucial for the neophyte because of the need to identify with the profession. It is also the time during which the new graduate is most vulnerable to influence. Conflicts emerge between ideology and reality in the work situation. The kind of empathy, guidance and support may well alter the remainder of the graduate's career (Kramer & Schmalenberg, 1978; McGrath & Koewing, 1978). In other professions, such as medicine and law, an internship is generally provided to enable the novice to work closely with an expert in the field. Expertise is gained by an emphatic relationship with the proctor or expert. The ability to problem solve without fear of failure is gained under close supervision and guidance. Immersing the novice in actual task environments where experts are engaged helps the beginner to apply the rules and procedures in practice (Broderick & Ammentorp, 1979). The human relations aspect of this novice-expert relationship is critical. The ability of the expert to empathize with the beginning practitioner is essential. If the expert is not empathetic, the results of the relationship may be detrimental, and cause more harm than good (LaMonica, Carew, Winder, Haase, & Blanchard, 1976).

Statement of the Hypothesis

The need for a new approach to the orientation of new graduate nurses emerges from 1) dissatisfaction of hospital administrators with the clinical experiences of new graduates, and 2) dissatisfaction on the part of new graduates with their first job experience as evidenced by high turnover rates. Training models from other professions suggest that an empathetic relationship with an expert can be an effective strategy for dealing with both problems. Therefore, it is hypothesized that new graduate nurses whose orientation program utilizes a preceptor as a major component exhibit higher performance levels than new graduate nurses in a traditional orientation program.

References

Broderick, M.E., & Amentorp, W.M. Information structures: An analysis of nursing performance. Nursing Research, 1979, 28 (2), 106-111.

Cantor, M.M. Associate degree: Education for what? Journal of Nursing Education, 1974, 13, 26-31.

Ciatiello, J. Expectations of the associate degree graduate: A director of nursing's point of view. Journal of Nursing Education, 1974, 13, 22-25.

Cowden, P.W. the changing nature of professional work and new sources of professional dissatisfaction: A look at nursing (Doctoral dissertation, Harvard University, 1977). Dissertation Abstracts International, 1978, 38, 3773A-5093A. (University Microfilms No. 7730686).

Cronin-Stubbs, D. Job satisfaction and dissatisfaction among new graduate staff nurses. Journal of Nursing Administration, 1977, 7 (10), 44-50.

Everly, G.S., & Falcione, R.L. Perceived dimensions of job satisfaction for staff registered nurses. Nursing Research, 1976, 25 (5), 346-348.

Herzberg, F. Work and the nature of man. New York: T.Y. Crowell, 1966.

Kramer, M., & Schmalenberg, C.E. Bicultural training and new graduate role transformation. Nursing Digest, 1978, 5 (4), 1-48.

LaMonica, E.L., Carew, D.K., Winder, A.E., Haase, A.M.B., & Blanchard, K.H. Empathy training as the major thrust of a staff development program. Nursing Research, 1976, 25 (6), 447-452.

Martin, B.W., & McAdory, D.J. Are AD clinical experiences adequate? Nursing Outlook, 1977, 25 (8), 502-505.

McCloskey, J.C. Influence of rewards and incentives on staff nurse turnover rate. Nursing Research, 1974, 23 (3), 239-247.

McGrath, B.J., & Koewing, J.R. A clinical preceptorship for new graduate nurses. Journal of Nursing Administration, 1978, 8 (3), 12-19.

Rines, A.R. Associate degree education: History, development, and rationale. Nursing Outlook, 1977, 25 (8), 496-502.

Sheridan, J.E., & Vredenburgh, D.J. Usefulness of leadership behavior and social power variables in predicting job tension, performance, and turnover of nursing employees. Journal of Applied Psychology, 1978, 63 (1), 89-95.

Note: Many of the above references were identified using Index Medicus and Cummulative Nursing Index.

The Comparative Effectiveness of Parent Aides

Versus Salaried Paraprofessionals in

The Kindergarten Classroom[4]

Introduction

Individualized instruction is a priority in education today. Many teachers, however, find it to be an impossibility due to class size and time consuming non-professional duties. Recognizing this problem, an increased number of trained and salaried paraprofessionals have been hired by school systems to free teachers of duties which do not require professional competency. In many schools, the lack of funds for trained and salaried paraprofessional aides has led administrators to organize pools of volunteer parents to aid teachers in achieving individualized instruction.

Statement of the Problem

The problem to be investigated in this study is the comparative effectiveness of the use of volunteer parents as teachers' aides versus salaried and trained paraprofessional aides in the kindergarten.

Review of the Literature

A relatively new career field in education has emerged in recent years -- the paraprofessional. The paraprofessional (auxiliary personnel, teacher aide) is being hired by school systems in increasing numbers to free teachers of non-professional tasks and thereby maximizing professional efficiency. The duties of paraprofessionals vary from school system to school system and indeed from class to class. According to surveys, paraprofessional duties are largely clerical in nature, but also include housekeeping and classroom management jobs (NEA, 1967). Duties of teachers and aides often overlap and it is becoming apparent that teacher aides are beginning to take on responsibility in cognitive fields (Johnson & Faunce, 1973).

Paraprofessionals now hired by school systems represent a variety of academic and socio-economic backgrounds. In some areas college experience is needed to qualify and in other areas people with limited experience are hired as a community service for on the job training (Elliot, 1972). Usually

---

[4]Based on a paper by J. S. Schumm, Florida International University, Miami, 1974.

paraprofessionals participate in some type of orientation or in-service training to prepare them for their duties, however at times this training is lacking or weak (Johnson & Faunce, 1972).

Although there is some debate about the accreditation of (Jacobson & Drije, 1972) and legal limits of (LeConte, 1973) paraprofessionals in the public school, there seems to be general satisfaction on the part of teachers and aides (Templeton, 1972). Most teachers in the country do not have aides as yet, but those who do indicate that paraprofessionals lend substantial assistance (NEA, 1967). Aides seem to have enthusiasm for their semi-professional position and are eager for the opportunity to learn new skills (Templeton, 1972). It is interesting to note that one survey indicated that teachers were anxious for school boards to hire paraprofessionals, but believed that this should not take precedence over professional salary improvement (NEA, 1967).

Although it may be years before the true effect of paraprofessional performance in the area of student achievement can be measured accurately, studies have indicated that paraprofessionals do indeed contribute to significant improvement of student achievement (Templeton, 1972; Brickell, 1971). However, the effect of paraprofessionals on student attitudes is yet uncertain and further research is needed in this area (Templeton, 1972).

In many schools, administrators and teachers recognize the contribution that paraprofessional aides make to the implementation of individualized instruction, but finances do not enable the hiring of additional staff. An increasing number of administrators, PTA's and indeed individual teachers are organizing pools of volunteer parents to aid teachers in the classroom (Hedges, 1973). Studies indicate that parent acceptance (Carroll, 1973) and parent/teacher communication (Medinnus & Johnson, 1970) have definite bearing upon the cognitive achievement of children. Indeed, according to Title I ESEA, parent participation is required in the operation of educational programs sponsored by the Title funds (Boutwell, 1971). Studies reveal that the use of parents as teacher aides results in significant student growth and achievement (Hedges, 1973).

Additional benefits of parental participation in the schools are better community relations, broadening of the school program, development of parent skills, and support for educational programs (Elliot, 1972). Perhaps the greatest disadvantages of using parents (as opposed to salaried paraprofessionals) as classroom aides are that, as in any volunteer program, parents may fail to show up and in addition it is hard to require parents to attend training sessions. However, the overall advantages of using parents in the classroom seem to outweigh these drawbacks (Hedges, 1973).

Statement of the Hypothesis

Although parent volunteers may lack the specialized training, mandatory attendance, continuity, and incentive of a salary of a paraprofessional, the parents do have a personal stake in the matter -- the achievement of their own children. What the parents may lack in training (and dependability at times) they make up in a multitude of specialized talents and enthusiasm. In addition, the enlistment of parents is much less expensive than adding additional staff members.

Considering that all of the above mentioned studies show that student achievement is improved with the presence of a salaried, trained paraprofessional or volunteer parents in the classroom, and considering the presence of a teacher aide in the classroom (either salaried or volunteer) enables professional teachers to perform with greater efficiency and improved morale, it is hypothesized that kindergarten students who have a volunteer parent pool assisting their teacher in the classroom will show comparable achievement to kindergarten students who have a salaried paraprofessional in their classroom.

References

Boutwell, W. D. Parent Participation. PTA Magazine, 1971, 65(30), 30.

Brickell, H. M., et al. Paraprofessional influence on student achievement and attitudes and paraprofessional performance outside the classroom in district decentralized ESEA Title I and New York State Urban Education Projects in the New York City Schools. New York: Institute for Educational Development, 1971 (ERIC, ED 057 136).

Carroll, A. D. Parent acceptance, self-concept and achievement of kindergarten children (Doctoral dissertation, Auburn University, 1973). Dissertation Abstracts International, 1973, 34, 2907A-2908A. (University Microfilms No. 73-31, 616).

Elliot, D. L. Parent participation in the elementary school. Richmond, Calif.: Richmond Unified School District, 1972 (ERIC, ED 071 751).

Hedges, H. G. Extending volunteer programs in schools. St. Catharines, Niagara Centre: Ontario Institute for Studies in Education, 1973 (ERIC, ED 085 846).

Jacobson, C., & Drije, C. Role relations between professionals and paraprofessionals in Head Start. Journal of Research and Development in Education, 1972, 5(2), 95-100.

Johnson, L., & Faunce, R. W. Teacher aides: A developing role. Elementary School Journal, 1973, 74(3), 136-144.

LeConte, M. J. The legal status of paraprofessionals in education (Doctoral dissertation, Miami University, 1973). Dissertation Abstracts International, 1973, 34, 1537A. (University Microfilms No. 73-24, 492).

Medinnus, G. R., & Johnson, T. M. Parental perceptions of
    kindergarten children. The Journal of Educational Re-
    search, 1970, 63(8), 379-381.
NEA Research Division. How the profession feels about
    teacher aides. NEA Journal, 1967, 56(8), 16.
Templeton, I. Paraprofessionals: Educational management re-
    view series number 11. Eugene, Oregon: Oregon Univer-
    sity, ERIC Clearinghouse on Educational Management, 1972
    (ERIC, ED 071 145).

Effects of a Play-Oriented Kindergarten
Curriculum on Academic Readiness[5]

Introduction

In recent years, an emphasis has been placed on academic achievement, cognitive learning, and preparation for the next grade level. Following the Russian launching of Sputnik, the public concluded that American schools had failed, and the question "What are we teaching our children?" was generated (Gallegos, 1983; Webster, 1984). This question placed great pressure on school systems to develop curricula which would accelerate the child's academic training and skills, with kindergarten becoming the first front in this "academic war".

As a result, no longer are kindergarteners allowed to merely interact with their peers and to explore the educational environment and the learning process. Rather, these five-year-olds are now receiving formal instruction, especially in the area of reading, from commercially produced structured programs and materials. Today's kindergarteners are expected to complete worksheets and participate in phonics lessons, and are held to long periods of controlled activities. These children participate in an academically oriented routine that was once expected of first graders (Ballenger, 1983; Gentile & Hoot, 1983).

For many educators, the issue is not whether these young children can be successfully taught, but rather whether this structured approach is truly beneficial to them. Many believe that kindergarteners were, in fact, better prepared for academic pursuits when they were allowed time to acquire judgment of symbols, develop a pattern of exploration, explore their environment, and experiment without risk of failure (Ballenger, 1983).

Statement of the Problem

The purpose of this study was to compare the effects of two curriculum models, a play-oriented curriculum and an academic readiness-oriented curriculum, with respect to the academic readiness of kindergarteners. A play-oriented curriculum was defined as a "curriculum emphasizing child-directed representations of symbols through activities in which constructive materials, imaginative sequences, and elements of language are used" (Wolfgang & Sanders, 1981). An academic readiness-oriented curriculum was defined as a highly structured curriculum stressing phonics instruction and utilization of workbooks.

Review of Related Literature

The academic readiness programs which are found in American kindergartens today have multiplied during the past two decades. This increase has come about because of the desire of educators, and society in general, to improve children's opportunities for academic success (May & Campbell, 1981). The concept of these readiness programs evolved during the 1920's and 1930's in an attempt to reduce the number of failures in the first and second grades. However, today the term readiness is not accepted by all educators.

---

[5]Based on a paper by D. G. Lane, Florida International University, Miami, 1985.

Some find the term too vague, while others feel that programs have become too rigid (May & Campbell, 1981), and view them as unwise attempts to accelerate the child's academic training and achievement (Johnson & Johnson, 1982).

Critics of academic readiness programs question whether five- or six-year-olds are cognitively ready for the complex decoding and abstracting processes required in learning how to read. Their criticism is based on research findings which conclude that it is not until the age of seven or eight that children develop the logical thinking ability which is essential in giving meaning to the written word (Johnson & Johnson, 1982). In addition, many educators perceive this type of early childhood program as an extension of the elementary school, where kindergarteners begin to receive formalized reading instruction which was once reserved for first graders (Elkind, 1982; Webster, 1984). Studies concerned with the optimal age at which early instruction should begin, early reading instruction in particular, have been conducted (Elkind, 1982). According to Johnson and Johnson (1982), a study conducted by Davis, Timble and Vincent found that children who started first grade at the age of six registered significantly higher scores on reading achievement tests than those who started at the age of five. A similar finding was reported by Feitelson, Tehori, and Levinberg-Green (1982), who worked with five- to seven-year-olds in Israel. These researchers reported that children who entered first grade at the age of six-and-one-half years or older scored significantly higher than those students who entered first grade at age six or younger. Other researchers have also questioned the value of early academic training because it does not appear to provide any permanent advantage to those young children who receive it (Davis, 1980; Johnson & Johnson, 1982; Webster, 1984).

Furthermore, in terms of academic learning from a Piagetian view, a child can not begin to comprehend reading material unless it reflects the child's existing knowledge. This knowledge must have been constructed from personal experiences with objects and through a variety of play activities (Raph, 1980). According to May and Campbell (1981), Maier states that Piaget stresses a number of developmental levels which the child must experience in order for learning to take place. If educators attempt to escalate learning without taking into account the child's developmental levels, it could result in the child's first learning experience being one of frustration. This may in turn cause children to associate future learning with frustration , something to be avoided (Davis, 1980; Gallegos, 1983).

A number of educators and psychologists do not necessarily disagree with the above, but believe that learning can be accelerated if instruction is appropriate to the child's level. They cite Bruner and his associates who claim that any subject can be taught to any child at any stage of development (Johnson & Johnson, 1982; May & Campbell, 1981). It is these educators and psychologists who have dominated the early childhood education movement. Based on their assertions, society has pressured schools into establishing structured reading programs for early childhood classes. These societal pressures evolved from over-anxious parents, administrators who have little or no academic training in early childhood education, and publishers with powerful salesmanship qualities (Davis, 1980; Elkind, 1982). In their zest to teach kindergarten children to read by mandating large segments of teaching time, and by requiring kindergarten teachers to use highly structured reading programs and materials, these parents and educators have failed to realize how this instruction severely limits the opportunities for these five-year-olds to engage in play activities which are also a vital part of learning (Gentile & Hoot, 1983).

Recent expansion of research in the area of play and its effects on learning firmly supports the theories that claim that there is a critical relationship among play, learning to read, and early reading achievement (Gentile & Hoot, 1983). According to Pellegrini (1980), Glickman, in an attempt to explain reasons for young children's declining achievement scores, hypothesized that this decline may be due to a decrease in the frequency and quality of children's play at both home and school. Based on the results of his research, Glickman found a positive relationship between preschoolers' ability to play and performance on cognitive achievement tests. To further develop Glickman's research, Pellegrini (1980) conducted a study on school-age children which resulted in similar findings. In addition, Gallegos (1983) conducted a study of kindergarteners in which half of the children were enrolled in classes that stressed learning through play activities, and half were enrolled in classes that emphasized learning through teacher-directed instruction. This study also generated data supporting the premise that play does have a significant influence on the mastery of academic readiness skills. Further, the study found that the play group exhibited additional growth gains over and above the direct instruction group in a majority of the performance areas.

Statement of the Hypothesis

Most of the research on kindergarten curricula has focused on reading instruction and achievement. The research has generally found that delaying formal instruction is more productive. Other research has demonstrated the positive effects of play on achievement, and there is some evidence that play is more effective than structured activities. Given the evidence for reading, and the absence of contradictory findings in other curriculum areas, it is hypothesized that kindergarten children who participate in a play-oriented curriculum will exhibit greater academic readiness skills at the end of kindergarten than kindergarten children who participate in an academic readiness-oriented curriculum.

References

Ballenger, M. (1983). Reading in Kindergarten. Childhood Education, 59, 186-187.

Davis, H. (1980). Reading pressures in the kindergarten. Childhood Education, 57, 76-79.

Elkind, D. (1982). Early education: Are young children exploited? A commentary on Feitelson, Tehori, and Levinberg-Green. Merrill-Palmer Quarterly, 28, 495-497.

Feitelson, D., Tehori, B. Z., & Levinberg-Green, D. How effective is early instruction in reading? Experimental evidence. Merrill-Palmer Quarterly, 28, 485-493.

Gallegos, M. (1983). Learning academic skills through play. (ERIC Document Reproduction Service No. ED 225 690)

Gentile, F. M., & Hoot, J. L. (1983). Kindergarten play: The foundation of reading. The Reading Teacher, 36, 436-439.

Johnson, B., & Johnson, C. (1982). Overplacement: Children to failure. USA Today, 110(2442), 52-54.

May, C. R., & Campbell, R. (1981). Readiness for learning: Assumptions and realities. Theory Into Practice, 20, 130-134.

Pellegrini, A. D. (1980). The relationship between kindergarteners' play and achievement in prereading language and writing. Psychology in the Schools, 17, 530-535.

Raph, J. B. (1980). A cognitive start in kindergarten: Theory-research review. (ERIC Document Reproduction Service No. ED 194 188)

Webster, N. K. (1984). The 5s and 6s go to school, revisited. Childhood Education, 60, 325-330.

Wolfgang, C. H., & Sanders, T. S. (1981). Defending young children's play as the ladder to literacy. Theory Into Practice, 20, 116-120.

Note: The format and style of this paper and its references reflects requirements of the third (latest) edition of the Publication Manual of the American Psychological Association.

PART THREE

RESEARCH PLANS

TASK 3

For the hypothesis which you have formulated, develop
the remaining components of a research plan for a
study which you would conduct in order to test your
hypothesis. Include the following:

Method
    Subjects
    Instruments
    Design
    Procedure
Data Analysis
Time Schedule

Following this discussion, five examples are presented which illustrate
the performance called for by Task 3. These examples represent tasks submitted by the same students whose Tasks for Part Two were previously presented; consequently, the research plans match the introductions. Keep in
mind that since you do not yet possess the necessary level of expertise, the
proposed activities described in your plan (and in the examples presented) do
not represent ideal research procedure. You should also be aware that research plans are usually much more detailed. The examples given, however, do
represent what is expected of you at this point.

The Effectiveness of the Use of Hand-Held
Calculators in Tenth Grade General Math Classes

Method

Subjects

Subjects will be selected from among those in the tenth grade at Sanderson High School, Wake County Public Schools, North Carolina, who do not pass the mathematics section of the North Carolina Competency Test. Sixty students will be selected and placed into one of two groups.

Instrument

Subjects will be tested at the beginning of the study and at the end of the study with a standardized test which measures computational skill.

Design

There will be two randomly formed groups of 30 each. Both groups will be pretested and posttested.

Procedure

In the Fall, students in the tenth grade who fail the mathematics portion of the North Carolina Competency Test will be identified. Sixty students will be randomly selected and randomly assigned to one of two classes. Both groups will be pretested to establish initial level of computational skill. For the duration of the school year, one class will utilize hand-held calculators in math instruction and the other class will not. Both classes will be taught by the same teacher and will use the same textbook. At the end of the school year both classes will be posttested to establish ending level of computational skill.

Analysis of Data

The scores of the calculator group and the non-calculator group will be compared using a t test. The score comparison will be made twice, once for pretest scores and once for posttest scores.

Time Schedule

Event	Beginning-Ending Date
Identification of students failing competency test and placement into groups	9/1 - 9/15
Pretesting	9/16
Math instruction with or without calculators	9/17 - 5/15
Posttesting	5/16
Analysis of scores	5/17 - 6/1
Report writing	10/1 - 7/1

Behavior Modification as an Alternative

To Amphetamine Therapy in Treating

Hyperkinesis in Children

Method

Subjects

The sample group for this study will be selected from
the population of South Side School, Carter County Center for
behaviorally disturbed, elementary-age children. Only those
children who have been diagnosed as "hyperkinetic" or "hyperactive" by a school psychologist will be considered as comprising the population. The method of sampling to be used
will be stratified sampling, with the ages from 6 through 10
represented in the sample. Forty-five subjects will be
selected, to be randomly assigned to three treatment groups.

Instrument

Pre- and posttest instruments will be the Porteus Maze
Test and the Becker Child Observation System.

Design

There will be three randomly formed groups. Each group
will be pretested and posttested.

Procedure

After they have been classified by age, subjects will
be randomly assigned to one of three treatments. All groups
will be pretested in January at the beginning of the second
semester. During the second semester behavior modification
techniques will be used with group 1, group 2 will receive
amphetamine therapy, and group 3 will follow regular classroom procedure. Each treatment procedure will take place in
a classroom setting, following the regular school hours and
schedule. The facilities of South Side School will be used.
Teachers of the three treatment groups will all have had a
minimum of three years experience in teaching behaviorally
disturbed children. The teacher of group 1 will take part
in a 20-hour training session in the specific behavior modification techniques to be used. All three treatment classrooms will follow the same academic curriculum, with teachers
responsible for individually programming each child.

It is assumed that all three teachers participating in the study will have the same degree of skill in individualizing instruction and programming appropriate academic tasks. It is further assumed that the individualized curriculum will prevent the age range in each classroom from being a factor influencing results.

A major limitation of the study is that results may not be generalized to populations larger than class size of 15, and to classrooms taught by teachers with no prior experience in teaching behaviorally disturbed youngsters. In May, at the end of the second semester, all subjects will be posttested.

Method of Analysis

The performance of the three groups will be compared using analysis of variance.

Time Schedule

	January	February	March	April	May	June
Assignment of subjects	____					
Pretesting	___					
Treatment		_____				
Posttesting					___	
Data analysis					_____	
Research report writing		_____				

The Effectiveness of the Use of Preceptors

In the Orientation of New Graduate Nurses

Method

Subjects

Subjects will be new graduate nurses employed by the Florida Medical Center. The hospital is a proprietary one with 400 acute care beds.

Instrument

The newly-employed graduate nurses will be tested before and after orientation with the Florida Medical Center Skills Inventory.

Design

New graduate nurses will be divided into two groups, an experimental group and a control group. Both groups will be pretested at the beginning of orientation and posttested at the conclusion of orientation.

Procedure

Before the study begins nurses on the staff at the Florida Medical Center will be selected to serve as preceptors. Selected nurses will receive training regarding the role of a preceptor. During the period of the study new graduate nurses will be assigned to either a preceptor or a traditional supervisor on an alternating basis. That is, the first, third, fifth, and so forth, nurse hired will be assigned to a trained preceptor and the second, fourth, sixth, and so forth, nurse hired will be assigned to a traditional supervisor. All newly hired nurses will be administered the Florida Medical Center Skills Inventory at the beginning and end of their official orientation.

Method of Analysis

The scores of the experimental and the control group will be compared using a t test.

Time Schedule

Activity	Date
Select preceptors	December, week 1
Train preceptors	December, week 3
Conduct study	January, week 1 -- September, week 4
Analyze data	October, week 1 -- October, week 3
Write research report	January, week 2 -- November, week 3

The Comparative Effectiveness of Parent Aides

Versus Salaried Paraprofessionals in

The Kindergarten Classroom

Method

Subjects

This study will take place at three Dade County schools; one using paraprofessional aides, one with a pool of parent-aides, and one with no teacher aides. The schools will all be located in an upper-middle class suburban section of the southwest area of Dade County and each will have 3 or 4 kindergarten classes, 30 students per class. Random cluster sampling will be used to select two classes from each of the three schools involved.

Instrument

All students will be pretested and posttested using an achievement test appropriate for preschool children.

Design

Six randomly selected classes will be included in this study. All groups will be pretested and posttested.

Procedure

Two classes will be randomly selected from each of three schools -- one school which uses paraprofessional aides, one which uses parent aides, and one which does not utilize aides. Although there are many terms used to refer to teacher aides (non-professionals, auxiliary personnel, paraprofessionals) for the sake of consistency in the study, the term parapro-fessional will be used to refer to the salaried, trained group of volunteer parents. At the beginning of the school year all students will be pretested. Parent aides will be required to attend two training sessions, one in September and one in January. The training sessions will be planned by teachers and administrators of the school. The parapro-fessionals will participate in an in-service training program designed by the teachers and administrators of the school. The curriculum for the six kindergarten classes will be standard and the groups will differ mainly with respect to whether the teachers have an aide or not, and if they do

whether the aide is a professional or not. A limitation of
this study is that the duties of teacher aides are not standardized from class to class. Depending on the professional
teacher in charge, the teacher aide may have clerical, housekeeping, classroom management, or even cognitive duties. However, it is being assumed that each teacher in the study will
assign duties to teacher aides which she feels will enable
her to make best use of her time and training as a professional in the classroom. At the end of the school year, all the
students will be posttested.

Data Analysis

The two groups within each school will be considered as
a single treatment. Thus the combined performance of the two
groups in each school will be compared to the combined performance of the groups in each of the other schools.

Time Schedule

Activity	Dates
Selection of subjects	August 15-30
Administration of pretest	September 15
Training of aides	September 1-15 January 15-30
Administration of posttest	June 15
Analysis of data	June 15-30
Preparation of report	Ongoing -- Completed by July 15

Effects of a Play-Oriented Kindergarten
Curriculum on Academic Readiness

Method

Subjects

Subjects for this study will be kindergarten children enrolled in a middle-class elementary school in Dade County, Florida. Two classes will be randomly selected to participate.

Instrument

Academic readiness will be measured using a standardized test of readiness skills appropriate for kindergarten children.

Design

There will be two randomly selected groups (classrooms). Both groups will be pretested and posttested.

Procedure

At the beginning of the school year, two of the anticipated four kindergarten classes will be randomly selected to be in the study. The two kindergarten teachers who are most alike with respect to education and experience will be assigned to the classes. The selected teachers will receive training appropriate to their group. Both classes will be administered a standardized academic readiness test. For the remainder of the school year, one class will participate in a play-oriented curriculum. Children in this class will be encouraged to explore their environment, manipulate concrete objects, and interact with their peers. The other class will participate in an academic readiness-oriented curriculum. Children in this group will engage in highly structured, teacher directed activities, and will utilize structured materials such as worksheets. At the end of the school year, both classes will be posttested using the same test as was used for pretesting.

Data Analysis

Respective gains in the readiness skills of the two classes will be compared using a t test.

Time Schedule

Activity	Date
Selection of Classes	9/5
Selection/Training of Teachers	9/5 - 9/9
Pretesting	9/12
Differential Curricula	9/13 - 5/28
Posttesting	5/29
Data Analysis	6/1 - 6/15
Report Preparation	9/15 - 7/15

PART FOUR

SUBJECTS

EXERCISES

The Enablers for Part Four involve descriptions of four sampling techniques and procedures for applying each technique. If you are going to be
tested on these enablers, do not memorize definitions. If you understand a
concept you should be able to explain it in your own words. If asked to explain random sampling, for example, you do not have to (and should not) quote
Part Four by saying "random sampling is the process of selecting a sample in
such a way that all individuals in the defined population have an equal and
independent change of being selected for the sample." Instead, you might say
"random sampling means that every subject has the same chance of being picked
and whether or not one subject gets picked has nothing to do with whether or
not any other subject gets picked." Your performance on Enablers 2,4, 6 and
7 may be evaluated through a testing situation which requires you to apply a
given sampling procedure to a given set of circumstances. In order to give
you practice in applying each of the techniques, a number of situations follow this discussion. Three examples are given for each of the four sampling
techniques. Do the first example for each technique; if your responses match
the Suggested Responses you are probably ready for an enabler test and for
Task 4. If you do any of the examples incorrectly, study the Suggested Response and then do the second example for that technique. If necessary, repeat the process with the third example.

List the procedures for using a table of random numbers to select a sample, given the following situations.

1. There are 150 first graders in the population and you want a random sample of 60 students.

   1) _____

    _____

    _____

   2) _____

    _____

    _____

   3) _____

    _____

    _____

   4) _____

    _____

    _____

   5) _____

    _____

    _____

   6) _____

    _____

    _____

2. There are 220 principals in the school system and you want a random sample of 40 principals.

1) _____

_____

_____

2) _____

_____

_____

3) _____

_____

_____

4) _____

_____

_____

5) _____

_____

_____

6) _____

_____

_____

3. There are 320 students defined as gifted in the school system and you want a random sample of 50 gifted students.

1) _____

_____

_____

2) _____

_____

_____

3) _____

_____

_____

4) _____

_____

_____

5) _____

_____

_____

6) _____

_____

_____

List the procedures for selecting a stratified sample, given the following situations.

1. There are 500 twelfth-grade students in the population, you want a sample of 60 students, and you want to stratify on three levels of IQ in order to insure equal representation.

1) _____

_____

_____

2) _____

_____

_____

2. There are 95 algebra I students in the population, you want a sample of 30 students, and you want to stratify on sex in order to insure equal representation of males and females.

1) _____

_____

_____

2) _____

_____

_____

3. There are 240 principals in the school system, you want a sample of 45 principals, and you want to stratify by level, i.e., elementary versus secondary, in order to insure proportional representation. You know that there are approximately twice as many secondary principals as elementary principals.

1) _____

   _____

   _____

2) _____

   _____

   _____

EXERCISE IV - 3

List the procedures for cluster sampling, given the following situations.

1. There are 80 sixth-grade classrooms in the population, each classroom has an average of 30 students, and you want a sample of 180 students.

1) _____

   _____

   _____

2) _____

   _____

   _____

3) _____

   _____

   _____

2. There are 75 schools in the school system, each school has an average of 50 teachers, and you want a sample of 350 teachers.

   1) _____

       _____

       _____

   2) _____

       _____

       _____

   3) _____

       _____

       _____

3. There are 100 kindergarten classes in the school system, each class has an average of 20 children, and you want a sample of 200 children.

   1) _____

       _____

       _____

   2) _____

       _____

       _____

   3) _____

       _____

       _____

List the procedures for selecting a systematic sample, given the following situations.

1. You have a list of 2000 high school students, and you want a sample of 200 students.

   1) _____

      _____

      _____

   2) _____

      _____

      _____

   3) _____

      _____

      _____

2. You have a directory which lists the names and addresses of 12,000 teachers and you want a sample of 2,500 teachers.

   1) _____

      _____

      _____

   2) _____

      _____

      _____

3) _____

_____

_____

3. You have a list of 1,500 junior high school
   students, and you want a sample of 100 students.

1) _____

_____

_____

2) _____

_____

_____

3) _____

_____

_____

PART FOUR

SUBJECTS

TASK 4

Having selected a problem, and having formulated one or
more testable hypotheses or answerable questions, describe a sample appropriate for evaluating your hypotheses or answering your questions. This description will
include:

a) a definition of the population from which the
   sample would be drawn;
b) the procedural technique for selecting the
   sample and forming the groups;
c) sample sizes; and
d) possible sources of sampling bias.

Task 4 involves descriptions of a population and the procedure for selecting a sample from that population. Following this discussion, **five** examples are presented which illustrate the performance called for by Task 4.
Again, these examples represent tasks submitted by the same students whose
Tasks 2 and 3 were presented. Consequently, the sampling plans represent
refinements of the ones included in Task 3.

The Effectiveness of the Use of Hand-Held

Calculators in Tenth Grade General Math Classes

Subjects for this study will be selected from among those tenth grade students at Sanderson High School who do not pass the mathematics portion of the North Carolina Competency Test. Sanderson High School is part of the Wake County Public School System and is located in Raleigh, North Carolina. Sixty subjects will be randomly selected (using a table of random numbers) and those 60 will be randomly assigned to one of two groups (also using a table of random numbers). The results of this study will be limited in their generalizability since only low-ability students will be involved, i.e., those who fail the math section of the competency test.

Behavior Modification as an Alternative

To Amphetamine Therapy in Treating

Hyperkinesis in Children

The sample group for this study will be selected from the population of South Side School, Carter County Center for behaviorally disturbed, elementary-aged children. Only those children who have been diagnosed as being "hyperkinetic" or "hyperactive" by a school psychologist will be considered as comprising the population for this study.

The population will be stratified according to age, i.e., 6, 7, 8, 9, and 10. The total sample size will be 45; 9 subjects will be randomly selected from each of the 5 age levels. Three subjects from each age level will then be randomly assigned to each of three treatment groups. Thus, each treatment group will be composed of 15 subjects, with the ages from 6 to 10 equally represented in each group.

Since the sample will be drawn from only one school, subjects may represent a rather limited population. However, the school does draw its student body from all students in Carter County.

The Effectiveness of the Use of Preceptors

In the Orientation of New Graduate Nurses

The sample for this study will be all new graduate nurses (N=50-60) employed by the Florida Medical Center between January 1 and June 30. Florida Medical Center is a proprietary hospital with 400 acute care beds, and is located in Fort Lauderdale, Florida. This hospital also serves as a clinical facility for professional nursing students, practical nursing students, respiratory therapists, physical therapists, unit secretaries, home health aides, and dietary technicians. It offers a varied and extensive educational program for its employees. The hospital tends to serve a middle to upper income clientele.

Since a maximum of 60 nurses is anticipated to be employed over the six-month period, stratified random sampling will be used to form the experimental (preceptor) group and control group. Of the numbers 1-10, 5 will be randomly selected to be experimental numbers and the remaining 5 will be control numbers. Of the numbers 11-20, 5 will be randomly selected to be experimental numbers, and the remaining 5 will be control numbers. Similarly, of the numbers 21-30, 31-40, 41-50 and 51-60, 5 of each set will be randomly selected to be experimental numbers. Thus, for example, when the 24th nurse is hired, it will already have been determined whether that nurse will be in the experimental group or the control group. Selecting 5 experimental subjects from each group of 10 will ensure that nurses hired at various points in time will be equally represented in the experimental and control groups. In other words, half of the first 10 nurses hired will be experimental and half will be control; half of the next 10 will be experimental and half control, and so forth.

The Comparative Effectiveness of Parent

Aides Versus Salaried Paraprofessionals

In the Kindergarten Classroom

The sample for this investigation will be selected from all 150 children enrolled in the kindergarten at an elementary school in Hudson County. The school is located in an upper-middle class suburban area of the county.

Sixty of the kindergarten children will be randomly selected (using a table of random numbers) and will then be randomly assigned (by flipping a coin) to one of two classrooms.

Effects of a Play-Oriented Kindergarten

Curriculum on Academic Readiness

The subjects for this study will be selected from the kindergarten population (approximately 100 students) enrolled at an elementary school in Dade County, Florida. The school is located in a middle class, suburban neighborhood. The children who attend the school are predominantly Nonhispanic Caucasian. Fifty of the kindergarten children will be randomly selected, using a table of random numbers, and will be randomly assigned to one of two classrooms. One of the classrooms will be randomly designated as the play-oriented classroom, and the other will be the academic readiness-oriented classroom.

PART FIVE

INSTRUMENTS

EXERCISES

The Enablers for Part Five involve descriptions of various types of validity and reliability, descriptions of the procedures for determining each, descriptions of types of tests, and procedures for selection and administration of tests. Again, if you are going to be tested on these enablers, do not try to memorize. Instead, see if you can explain each concept in your own words; if you can, you probably will retain the concepts much better and will be able to explain them in a testing situation. Exercises V-1 and V-2 will assist you in understanding the basic concepts of validity and reliability.

Your performance on Enablers 4 and 6 may be evaluated through a testing situation which requires you to apply a given procedure for establishing validity to a given set of circumstances. In order to give you practice in applying each of the procedures, a number of situations are presented in Exercises V-3 and V-4. Three examples are given for each procedure; if your responses match the Suggested Responses, you are probably ready for an enabler test. If you do either of the examples incorrectly, study the Suggested Response and then do the second example for that procedure. If necessary, repeat the procedure with the third example.

Match each statment with the appropriate type of validity by placing the letter corresponding to the type of validity on the blank in front of each statement.

_____ 1. Requires item validity and sampling validity.

_____ 2. Is of prime importance for an aptitude test.

_____ 3. Permits substitution of a shorter test for a longer test.

_____ 4. Is most important for an achievement test.

_____ 5. Would be of concern to a developer of a test of aspirations.

A. content
B. construct
C. concurrent
D. predictive

EXERCISE V - 2

Match each statement with the appropriate type of reliability by placing the letter corresponding to the type of reliability on the blank in front of each statement.

_____ 1. Requires a correction formula.

_____ 2. Estimates stability of scores over time.

_____ 3. Estimates degree to which two tests measure the same thing.

_____ 4. In general, the best estimate of reliability.

_____ 5. When corrected, tends to over-estimate reliability.

A. test-retest
B. equivalent-forms
C. split-half
D. rationale equivalence

List procedures for determining concurrent validity, given the following situations.

1. You want to determine the concurrent validity of a new IQ test for young children.

   1) _____
   _____
   _____

   2) _____
   _____
   _____

   3) _____
   _____
   _____

   4) _____
   _____
   _____

2. You want to determine the concurrent validity of a new self-concept scale for junior high school students.

   1) _____
   _____
   _____

2) _____

_____

_____

3) _____

_____

_____

4) _____

_____

_____

3. You want to determine the concurrent validity of a new reading comprehension test for high school students.

1) _____

_____

_____

2) _____

_____

_____

3) _____

_____

_____

4) _____

_____

_____

List procedures for determining predictive validity, given the following situations.

1. You want to predict success in graduate school and you want to determine the predictive validity of the GRE.

    1) _____
       _____
       _____

    2) _____
       _____
       _____

    3) _____
       _____
       _____

    4) _____
       _____
       _____

2. You want to predict level of achievement in algebra I and you want to determine the predictive validity of an algebra I aptitude test.

    1) _____
       _____
       _____

2) _____

_____

_____

3) _____

_____

_____

4) _____

_____

_____

3. You want to predict success in nursing school and you want to determine the predictive validity of a nursing aptitude test.

1) _____

_____

_____

2) _____

_____

_____

3) _____

_____

_____

4) _____

_____

_____

INSTRUMENTS

TASK 5

Having stated a problem, formulated one or more hypotheses or questions, and described a sample, describe three
instruments appropriate for collection of data pertinent
to the hypothesis or question. For each instrument selected, the description will include:

a) the name, publisher and cost;
b) a description of the instrument;
c) validity and reliability data;
d) the type of subjects for whom
   the instrument is appropriate;
e) instrument administration
   requirements;
f) training requirements for scoring;
   and
g) a synopsis of reviews.

Based on these descriptions, indicate which test is
most acceptable for your "study" and why.

Task 5 involves description and comparative analysis of three measuring
instruments appropriate for collection of data pertinent to your hypothesis.
Since the task is relatively straightforward, only one example which illustrates the performance called for by Task 5 will be presented.

The Comparative Effectiveness of Parent Aides

Versus Salaried Paraprofessionals in

The Kindergarten Classroom

Test 1 (from Buros, 7th Yearbook, #17)

a) Peabody Individual Achievement Test (PIAT)
Lloyd M. Dunn and Frederick C. Markwardt, Jr.
American Guidance Service, Inc.
$24 per set of test materials and 25 record booklets
Postage extra

b) A description -- an individual test with 1 form, with testing time of 30-40 minutes. The PIAT has five subtests
(mathematics, reading comprehension, reading recognition,
spelling and general information) and yields six scores
(each of the five subtest scores plus a total).

c) Reliability: Test-retest reliabilities, based on a one-
month interval, are presented for the total test (.82 to
.92, median .89) and each of the subtests: mathematics
(.52 to .84, median, .74), reading recognition (.81 to
.94, median .88), reading comprehension (.61 to .78,
median .64), spelling (.42 to .78, median .65), and
general information (.70 to .88, median .76). The reading
recognition subtest has very nearly as much reliability
as the total test. More confidence can be placed in the
total score than in the subtest scores. Correlations between PIAT and PPVT IQ's range from .53 to .79 with median
.68. Validity: 7th Yearbook states no quantitative data
on validity, however one reviewer offers the general
statement that the PIAT "demonstrated less validity" than
its group achievement test competitors.

d) Grades kgn -- 12

e) No formal training is required to administer the PIAT,
however non-professional test administrators should be
carefully instructed before using the instrument. Directions are clearly stated, but the cautions and limita-
tions set by the authors must be carefully followed if the
test is to be administered meaningfully.

f) No specific training requirements were mentioned.

g) PIAT is an adequate instrument for quick, generalized
screening of achievement in the areas of mathematics,
reading, spelling, and general information. Because it is
designed for a wide age span, 5 subtests, and limited testing time, it is not a test for specific and comprehensive
achievement testing. PIAT does not include subtests for
science, social studies or study skills. Perhaps the most
impressive feature of PIAT is its attractive format. The
reviewers agree that PIAT has the potential for being a

well-accepted tool for quick, rough estimate of educational levels, but that more research and revision is
needed for improvement in regard to its validity and subtest reliability.

Test 2 (from Buros, 7th Yearbook, #33)

a) Tests of Basic Experiences (TOBE)
   Margaret H. Moss
   McGraw-Hill
   $32.50 per 30 sets of the battery
   $9.00 per 30 copies of any one test in the battery
   $9.25 per 30 general concepts tests
   Postage extra
   $3.00 per specimen set
   Scoring service, $2.25 per battery of 4 tests
   Spanish edition available

b) A description -- a group test with 2 levels (prekinder-
   garten -- kindergarten and kindergarten -- grade 1), one
   form each. TOBE is designed to test the "richness of conceptual background" of children in preschool, kindergarten,
   or first grade. Each of the two levels has four separate
   tests -- mathematics, language, science, and social
   studies -- and one composite test of general concepts
   which includes items from the other four. Each test con-
   tains 28 items and requires approximately 25 minutes to
   administer.

c) Reliability: No information is given in the 7th Yearbook.
   Validity: The procedure used to determine the content
   of the test is a combination of norm-referenced and cri-
   terion-referenced criteria. The manual states, "Items
   were selected to achieve a balance which avoided very easy
   and very difficult items (norm-referenced) but some items
   which appeared to be relatively easy or relatively difficult were retained due to the desirability of a measure
   of the concept inherent in the items (criterion-refer-
   enced)." In selecting the items "every attempt was made
   to minimize the number of items based strictly on a knowledge of factual information and to maximize the number
   of items based on a child's understanding of educationally relevant concepts." However, the reviewer suggests
   that many of the test items are not valid reflections of
   this data due to non-universal customs, esoteric information, and moralizing.

d) The grade level range for subjects is given as prekinder-
   garten -- grade 1, however the manual gives no information
   on the age range or other characteristics of the "prekin-
   dergarten children."

e) Proctors are required to assist with the administration of
   this examination. Although there are no other specific
   administration requirements, the reviewer suggests that
   the teacher teach behaviors such as "mark the" and "turn

the page" in sessions prior to the administration of the test.

f) No specific training requirements were mentioned.

g) In general the reviewer seemed pleased with the design of TOBE and noted that the administration procedures were very good for use with young children. The major drawback seems to be in the content of some test items. The reviewer also projected widespread use of this test due to the lack of tests for this age range for young children of widely different cultural backgrounds.

Test 3 (from Buros, 7th Yearbook, #28)

a) Stanford Early School Achievement Test (SESAT)
Richard Madden and Eric F. Gardner
Harcourt Brace Jovanovich, Inc.
$9.00 per 35 tests
$1.10 per scoring key and practice sheet
$1.50 per specimen set
scoring service, $1.50 and over per test

b) A description -- a group test with 2 levels (kindergarten-grade 1 and grade 1.0 - 1.5), one form each. The test is designed to appraise "the child's cognitive abilities. . . upon entrance into kindergarten, at the end of kindergarten, or upon entrance to the first grade." The test consists of four parts: Environment, Mathematics, Letters and Sounds, and Aural Comprehension. It yields five scores, one for each subtest plus a total score. The testing time is 90 minutes divided into five sessions.

c) Reliability: Split-half reliabilities range from .76 to .85. The intercorrelations among part and total scores range from .53 to .90. At the beginning of kindergarten the reliabilities range from .76 for scores on Aural Comprehension to .85 for scores on Environment. The other two subtests have reliabilities of .79. At the beginning of grade 1, the reliabilities are .77 for Aural Comprehension, .82 for Environment and for Mathematics, and .89 for Letters and Sounds.
Validity: The manual gives no specific information regarding procedures used to determine the content of the test. Although reviewers state that the items appear to have both face and content validity, they felt that more specific information should have been presented by the authors concerning the item analysis program.

d) Form 1: kindergarten -- grade 1
Form 2: grade 1 -- grade 1.5

e) No formal training is required to administer the SESAT, and the manual instructions are clear and specific.

f) No special training required.

g) The reviewers agree that SESAT is a well-constructed instrument to aid teachers in determining where to begin (what level) their instruction of the students. The test is of moderate reliability with better than average format, directions, and item quality. The test offers good suggestions for the teacher in using the data to design the classroom curriculum.

From my review of the above mentioned tests I have come to the following conclusions:

1. Buros' 7th Yearbook listed very few achievement batteries for kindergarten use. Those that were described were not comparable in reliability and validity with achievement tests for other age levels. With the increasing emphasis on early childhood education more achievement batteries will soon be available (according to an article I read in the Review of Educational Research). However, after reviewing the tests currently available, I decided to choose the three tests mentioned above for investigation.

2. The Peabody Individual Achievement Test (PIAT) is considered to be an exceptionally attractive test in regard to format, however the content is designed only to determine the general level of achievement. I feel that for this experiment, I need a more specific instrument.

3. The PIAT is an individually administered test and I feel that it would take too much time to administer the test to my sample. PIAT is designed for quick screening of individual students (such as transfer students).

4. The Tests of Basic Experiences (TOBE) did not state validity and reliability figures.

5. I was impressed with the administration procedures for the TOBE and felt that procedure-wise it was most suited to kindergarten children.

6. Overall, I feel that the Stanford Early School Achievement Test is the most suited for this study. Although the reliability is described as "average," I could not find a test for kindergarten level with much higher reliability.

7. The Stanford test is relatively inexpensive and is administered to a group, which would take less time from the classroom situation.

8. According to Buros' 7th Yearbook, Stanford Achievement Tests are the "patriarch" of achievement tests. The most "widely used over the longest period." Reviewers called for more research in regard to the PIAT and TOBE.

PART SIX

RESEARCH METHODS AND PROCEDURES

EXERCISES

Read each of the statements following the list of threats to validity. For each statement, identify the threat represented and place its letter in the blank in front of each description.

A. history
B. maturation
C. testing
D. instrumentation
E. statistical regression

F. differential selection
G. mortality
H. selection-maturation interaction, etc.
I. pretest-treatment interaction

J. selection-treatment interaction
K. specificity of variables
L. reactive arrangements

1. _____ A number of students in the experimental after-school fitness program dropped out when baseball season began.
2. _____ The treatment group behaved very well because the observers were recording their behavior.
3. _____ The first-grade students in the reading program being evaluated were also receiving perceptual-motor training in their physical education classes.
4. _____ The 30 students with the lowest scores on the multiple-choice vocabulary test were selected for participation in a remedial program.
5. _____ The students discussed the questions following administration of the pretest on American literature.

EXERCISE VI - 2

Read each of the statements following the list of designs. For each statement, identify the most appropriate design and place its letter on the blank in front of the statement.

A. pretest-posttest control group
B. posttest-only control group
C. nonequivalent control group
D. time series

E. one-group pretest-posttest
F. static group comparison
G. single-subject

1. _____ The population is emotionally disturbed children in need of self-control education.
2. _____ Our grant requires that we show that our approach improved the co-ordination of each participant.
3. _____ Random assignment is possible and we will be measuring computation ability after nine months of participation in one of two curricula.
4. _____ Students are already in classes. We will compare the social studies achievement of students in classes using Learning Activities Packages with the achievement of students in classes using the usual textbook and materials.
5. _____ We have randomly assigned students to 12 physical education classes - 6 coed classes, 3 all male classes, and 3 all female classes - and we will be measuring feelings concerning coeducational physical education classes.

PART SIX

RESEARCH METHODS AND PROCEDURES

TASK 6

> Having stated a problem, formulated one or more hypothe-
> ses, described a sample, and selected one or more measur-
> ing instruments, develop the method section of a research
> report. This should include a definition of subjects,
> instrument(s), research design, and specific procedures.

Task 6 involves development of the method section of your research report.
The examples which follow were prepared by the same students who prepared previous examples and you therefore should be able to see how Task 6 builds on
previous Tasks. Keep in mind that Tasks 3, 4 and 5 will not appear in your
final research report; Task 6 will. Therefore, each of the important points
in those previous tasks should be included in Task 6. Since earlier it was
recommended that you design an experimental study, the five examples all represent experimental research. If your study represents one of the other
methods of research, you should be able to generalize from the following
examples.

The Effectiveness of the Use of Hand-Held

Calculators in Tenth Grade General Math Classes

Method

Subjects

The sample for this investigation was selected from all 95 tenth-grade students at Sanderson High School (Wake County Public Schools, North Carolina) who did not pass the mathematics protion of the North Carolina Competency Test in the Fall of 1977. Sixty of the students were randomly selected (using a table of random numbers) and randomly placed into one of the four classes participating in the eight-month study.

Instrument

The Mathematics Computation section of the California Achievement Tests, Level 18C, was selected as the pretest-posttest instrument. The test was administered to the groups comprising each class and was timed, lasting 25 minutes. The test measured achievement with respect to the four basic arithmetic operations on integers, decimals, and fractions. Ten items appeared on the test for each of the four operations. The split-half reliability coefficient reported by the publisher approximated .96. The test was chosen because it meets the requirements of its purpose in the study. It is an instrument which measures computational knowledge as opposed to concepts or applications.

Experimental Design

The design used in this study was the pretest-posttest control group design (See Figure 1). This design was selected because of the feasibility of randomization and the need to obtain information on the students' computational achievement at the beginning of the study. While pretest-treatment interaction is a source of invalidity characteristic to this particular design, possible lack of generalization was believed to be minimized due to the duration of the study (eight months) and the apparent nonrelation of the pretest (in computational skills) and the treatment (calculator use) by the students.

Procedure

The 60 randomly selected students were randomly assigned to one of four classes, class I, II, III, or IV. After the classes were formed, they were randomly selected as control or experimental groups, two of each were to be formed in order to limit class size. The result of the random selections was:

Class I   Teacher A.   Treatment group
                                 (Calculator usage)   (n=15)

```
Class II      Teacher A.      Control group
                              (Non-calculator usage) (n=15)

Class III     Teacher B       Treatment group
                              (Calculator usage)     (n=15)

Class IV      Teacher B       Control group
                              (Non-calculator usage) (n=15)
```

GROUP A		PRETEST	TREATMENT	POSTTEST
Calculator Use n=30 (15 from class I, 15 from class III)	RANDOM ASSIGNMENT	CAT: MC*	Calculator Usage plus Regular Program	CAT: MC*

GROUP B		PRETEST	TREATMENT	POSTTEST
Non-calculator Use n=30 (15 from class II, 15 from class IV)	RANDOM ASSIGNMENT	CAT: MC*	Regular Instruction-al Program	CAT: MC*

*California Achievement Tests: Mathematics Computation

Figure 1. Experimental design.

The two teachers involved in the study taught one treatment and one control group each and had more than three years experience teaching high school remedial math courses using the text and curriculum guide supplied for the course by the school district. Shortly after the classes were formed, all students in the sample took the California Achievement Test: Mathematics Computation[1]. Scores were recorded and filed. The pretest scores were also used to prescribe individualized learning activities for all students. Calculators were not used on the pretest by any student.

The treatment groups shared the use of 15 hand-held electronic calculators throughout the year. They were given a three day instructional unit on the proper care and use of the calculator. The calculators used performed the four basic operations, provided a full floating decimal, a clear-last-entry button, an all-clear button, and a six-digit display. The calculators were operated with batteries, a supply of which was kept on hand. The set of 15 calculators was shared by the two treatment groups which met at different times of the day.

Subsequent to the initial three day calculator orientation session, each student in the treatment group was scheduled to work with the calculator for a minimum of 45 minutes per week. Schedules and Time Sheets were maintained

---

[1]CTB/McGraw-Hill. California Achievement Tests. Monterey, CA: Author, 1977.

by the teachers in order to maximize compliance with the established guidelines. The students used the calculators for a variety of purposes such as (1) checking answers to problems done by themselves and other students using paper and pencil, (2) computation on worksheets distributed by the instructor, (3) enrichment activities, and (4) correcting errors on teacher-made tests returned to the students.

The control groups were not denied anything other than the use of calculators. Verbal and reinforcement techniques were employed. Enrichment activities, although different from those experienced by the treatment groups, were not absent. Correction of errors on teacher-made tests was required. All four classes used the same textbook and followed the same curriculum guide.

Two weeks before the end of the academic year, the California Achievement Test: Mathematics Computation, Form 18C, was administered as the posttest to all students and scores were recorded alongside the corresponding pretest scores.

Behavior Modification as an Alternative to

Amphetamine Therapy in Treating

Hyperkinesis in Children

Method

Subjects

The sample group for this study was selected from the
population of South Side School, a center for behaviorally
disturbed youngsters which draws its student body from all
elementary schools in Carter County. All children in the
sample group had been diagnosed as being "hyperkinetic" or
"hyperactive" by a school psychologist prior to their place-
ment at South Side. Forty-five subjects comprised the
sample group, which was stratified according to age, with the
age levels from six through ten equally represented.

Instrument

The pretest and posttest instrument selected was the
Porteus Maze Test, which has been shown in various studies to
be a valid and reliable measure of impulsivity and the
ability to sustain attention and concentration. It has also
been shown to be a reliable indicator of drug effect, dis-
criminating between those hyperactive children on medication
and those not taking drugs (Burleigh, 1971). Thus, this
instrument was selected to measure three factors of the definition of hyperkinesis: impulsivity, impaired attention
span, and poor powers of concentration.

Research Design

The design utilized in this study was the pretest,
posttest, control group design (see Figure 1). Three treatment groups were formed: Group 1, behavior modification
techniques; Group 2, amphetamine treatment; and Group 3,
control, to use regular classroom procedures. This design
was chosen because it was considered essential to obtain a
pre-treatment measure of hyperactivity in order to reliably
evaluate the effects of the treatments. And, since five
months elapsed between pre- and posttesting, possible interaction of testing and treatment was not considered to be a
major threat to the external validity of the study.

Groups		Pretest	Treatment	Posttest
Group 1 n = 15	R	Porteus Maze Test	Behavior Modification	Porteus Maze Test
Group 2 n = 15	R	Porteus Maze Test	Amphetamine therapy	Porteus Maze Test
Group 3 n = 15	R	Porteus Maze Test	Usual class-room proce-dures	Porteus Maze Test

Figure 1. The experimental design.

Procedure

Nine subjects were randomly selected from each of the five age groups 6, 7, 8, 9, and 10, using a table of random numbers. Then, three subjects from each age group were randomly assigned into one of the treatment groups. Thus, each treatment group comprised 15 subjects, with the ages 6 through 10 equally represented.

After the subjects were selected, they were administered the Porteus Maze Test as a pre-treatment measure of hyperactivity. Three vacant classrooms at South Side School were set up and utilized as the setting for the treatment procedures. Regular school schedule and hours were observed. Treatment conditions began on January 13, 1974.

Teachers of the groups all had had at least three years experience in teaching behaviorally disturbed children. The teacher of Group 1 took part in a 20-hour training session in the specific behavior modification techniques that were to be used. All three treatment classrooms followed the same academic curriculum, with the teachers individually programming each child. The treatments were as follows:

Group 1, behavior modification: The check-card system was employed, with each child receiving check marks for completion of academic tasks, in-seat behavior, working quietly, and other appropriate classroom behaviors. The system was organized so that each child could earn up to 100 checks per day. Earned checks were traded in at the end of each day for tangible prizes which included candy, comic books, and small toys. Inappropriate behavior was ignored unless it endangered the child or others, in which case the time-out procedure was used (the child was removed to a small, bare, adjacent room for a specified period of time, not to exceed ten minutes).

Group 2, amphetamine treatment: The physician
assigned to South Side School examined each child
in Group 2 and prescribed an appropriate dosage
of medication. The physician was available for
the duration of the study to follow up and revise
dosages as necessary.

Group 3, the control group: Regular classroom
management procedures and techniques were
followed.

On May 19, 1974, the Porteus Maze Test was re-administer-
ed to all subjects, as a post-treatment measure of hyperactivity level.

The Effectiveness of the Use of Preceptors

In the Orientation of New Graduate Nurses

Method

Subjects

The subjects for the study were 52 new graduate nurses employed by the Florida Medical Center between January 1, 1980 and June 30, 1980. Florida Medical Center is a proprietary hospital with 400 acute care beds, and is located in Fort Lauderdale, Florida. This hospital also serves as a clinical facility for professional nursing students, practical nursing students, respiratory therapists, physical therapists, unit secretaries, home health aides and dietary technicians. It offers a varied and extensive educational program for its employees. The hospital tends to serve a middle to upper income clientele.

The 52 graduate nurses did not represent a cross section of nurses since 32 (61.5 percent) were foreign born (30 from the Phillipines and 2 from Cuba). Three (5.8 percent) were male, 40 (77 percent) were single, and ages ranged from 21 to 35. Thirty-four (65.4 percent) of the nurses were prepared at the baccalaureate level, 15 (28.8 percent) at the ADN level, and 3 (5.8 percent) at the diploma level. All foreign born nurses had taken the TOEFL (Test of English as a Foreign Language) before coming to the United States and had earned a passing score.

Instrument

The Florida Medical Center Skill Inventory was utilized as the pretest and posttest instrument to assess beginning practioner level of performance, as perceived by the graduate nurse. The Inventory is competency oriented and includes skills validated by the National League for Nursing (NLN). The skills included are ones which virtually all hospitals require. The instrument has been used by the Florida Medical Center for all of its nursing employees for the past six years and has been periodically revised as necessary. Validity and reliability studies were conducted by the NLN prior to initial use of the instrument.

Experimental Design

The design utilized in this study was the pretest-posttest control group design (See Figure 1). This design was selected because of the controls which it provides for sources of invalidity. The only major threat to validity associated with this design is possible pretest-treatment interaction, which may limit generalizability of results. This potential threat was assumed to be minimized in this study, however, because of the nonreactive nature of the pretest, the fact that use of the pretest instrument is routine at the Center, and the fact that 12 weeks intervened between pretesting and posttesting.

Group	Pretest	Treatment	Posttest
Experimental n-26	FMCSI*	Preceptor Orientation	FMCSI
Control n=26	FMCSI	Traditional Orientation	FMCSI

* Florida Medical Center Skills Inventory

Figure 1. Experimental design.

Procedure

Since a maximum of 60 new graduate nurses were anticipated to be included in the study, 30 registered nurses (RNs) were selected to serve as preceptors. Of the 518 nursing employees, 165 were RNs. Of the 165 RNs, those were identified who met the criteria for an effective preceptor: outstanding expertise in nursing, ability to communicate and teach, and empathy. Of those who met the criteria, 60 were randomly selected and randomly divided into two groups of 30 each, 30 preceptors and 30 controls. Although participation as a preceptor was strictly voluntary, all selected RNs willingly agreed to function in their assigned role. Selection of 30 preceptors ensured that no preceptor would have more than two new graduate nurses at any point in time. Within each group of 30, the RNs were randomly assigned a number from 1 to 30. This was done to enable assignment of RNs to newly employed graduate nurses on a random basis. Thus, the RN assigned the number 1 in the preceptor group was automatically assigned to the first graduate nurse employed in the preceptor group.

A two-day training experience was conducted for preceptors. A preceptor was defined as a professional who serves as a role model and a resource person for a new graduate. It was explained that a preceptor does not act as an instructor, per se, but is available as assistance is sought by the graduate. Hypothetical situations and simulation games were presented and the preceptors described how they would handle the various situations. Their responses were critiqued and they were assisted as needed. It was emphasized that the graduates were to initiate, pursue and evaluate their own learning activities with the preceptors' guidance and direction when requested. Preceptors were also told that if they perceived a potentially dangerous situation, they should intervene (as they normally would) rather than allow the graduate to practice unsafely.

Since a maximum of 60 nurses was anticipated to be employed over a six-month period, stratified random sampling was used to form the experimental (preceptor) group and the control group. Of the numbers 1-10, 5 were randomly selected to be experimental numbers and the remaining 5 were control numbers. Of the numbers 11-20, 5 were randomly selected to be experimental numbers, and the remaining 5 were control numbers. Similarly, of the numbers 21-30, 31-40, 41-50 and 51-60, 5 of each set were randomly selected to be experimental numbers. Thus, for example, when the 24th graduate nurse was hired, it was already determined that that nurse would be in the experimental group.

Selecting 5 experimental subjects from each group of 10 ensured that nurses hired at various points in time would be equally represented in the experimental and control groups. In other words, half of the first 10 graduate nurses hired were experimental and half control; half of the next 10 were experimental and half control, and so forth. During the six-month period, 52 graduate nurses were hired, 26 experimental nurses and 26 control nurses.

As each graduate nurse was hired, he/she was administered the Florida Medical Center Skills Inventory and was assigned to either a preceptor or a traditional supervisor. All new graduates worked in either the medical or surgical area and none was assigned to a specialty area (e.g., intensive care). The graduates worked the same days and hours as their preceptors or supervisors. From time to time the Director of Nursing Education held informal mini-conferences with the graduates, preceptors and supervisors in order to attempt to detect any personality conflicts. The graduates were unaware of their participation in a study and the intended differential nature of their supervision. At the conclusion of a 12-week orientation period, each graduate nurse was again administered the Florida Medical Center Skills Inventory. Since the last subject was hired during the last week of the selected 6-month period, and since orientation lasted 12 weeks, the actually study (exclusive of preceptor training) was conducted over a 9-month period. At the conclusion of the study, the pretest and posttest scores of the experimental group and the control group were compiled.

The Comparative Effectiveness of Parent Aides

Versus Salaried Paraprofessionals in

The Kindergarten Classroom

Method

Subjects

The sample for this investigation was selected from all 120 children enrolled in the kindergarten level at an elementary school in Hudson County. This school is located in the upper-middle class, suburban southwest area of the County. Sixty of the kindergarten children were randomly selected (using a table of random numbers) and were then randomly assigned to one of the two classrooms participating in this nine-month study.

Instrument

The Stanford Early School Achievement Test (SESAT) -- Level 1 was selected and used as the data gathering instrument for this study. Although the reliability and validity for this battery were described as "average," it did compare favorably with other achievement tests now available for the kindergarten level. The format, directions for administration, and price also compared positively with other early childhood achievement batteries. The SESAT consists of four parts (Environment, Mathematics, Letters and Sounds, and Aural Comprehension) and yields five scores, one for each subtest plus a total score. The testing time is 90 minutes, divided into 5 sessions. In general, the SESAT meets the demands of an instrument of measurement for this investigation in that it is a group administered test which is designed to appraise cognitive abilities of children upon entrance into and/or completion of kindergarten.

Experimental Design

The design used in this study was the pretest-posttest control group design (See Figure 1).

This design was selected because of the feasibility of randomization, the need to check for initial equivalency of the two groups, and the desire to obtain information on the cognitive abilities of each child at the beginning of the study. While this design controls quite well for sources of internal invalidity, external validity may be weakened due to pretest-treatment interaction. This potential problem, however, was believed to be minimized in this study because of the age and naïveté of the subjects and the duration of the study (nine months).

		PRETEST	TREATMENT	POSTTEST
GROUP A				
Parent-Aide n=30 (15 from CLASS 1 and 15 from CLASS 2	RANDOM ASSIGNMENT	Stanford Early School Achievement Test	Regular Instructional Program Plus Parent-Aide	Stanford Early School Achievement Test
GROUP B				
Paraprofessional Aide n=30 (15 from CLASS 1 and 15 from CLASS 2)	RANDOM ASSIGNMENT	Stanford Early School Achievement Test	Regular Instructional Program Plus Paraprofessional Aide	Stanford Early School Achievement Test

Figure 1. Experimental design.

Procedure

The 60 randomly selected students were randomly assigned to one of two classes, Class 1 or Class 2. After being assigned to a class, the students were randomly placed in one of the two experimental groups by tossing a coin. Therefore, the organization of this study was:

GROUP 1-A   Teacher 1, Treatment A
                    (parent aide) (n = 15)

GROUP 1-B   Teacher 1, Treatment B
                    (paraprofessional aide) (n = 15)

GROUP 2-A   Teacher 2, Treatment A
                    (parent aide) (n = 15)

GROUP 2-B   Teacher 2, Treatment B
                    (paraprofessional aide) (n = 15)

The two teachers involved in the study each had more than five years teaching experience and had recently participated in a workshop on individualized instruction sponsored by the school. The established program for instruction was not altered. The classroom teachers carried out programs in the usual manner.

Parent-aide pools were organized by the administration. Five parent aides (one scheduled for each morning of the week) plus two on-call alternates were assigned to Class 1 and Class 2. Parents were asked to be on duty between 9 a.m. and 12 p.m. on their assigned day. Parents were also required to attend training sessions held in September and January. The sessions were planned by the administrators and teachers in cooperation with the researcher. Paraprofessional aides were hired for both Class 1 and Class 2. The paraprofessional aides worked five days a week from 9 a.m. - 12 p.m. All aides participated in an inservice training program organized by the administrator and teachers in cooperation with the re-searcher.

At the beginning of the school year, the Stanford Early School Achievement Test was administered to all subjects. The tests were conducted in the individual classrooms. All scores were recorded on file cards and stored.

Duties of the parent aides and paraprofessional aides were identical. The aides were assigned to work with 1-5 children at a time -- the assignment being determined by teacher evaluation of student needs. Responsibilities in-cluded grading papers, assisting absentees with make-up work, aiding with enrichment activities for advanced students and aiding in remedial instruction as needed. Specific instruc-tions were given by the teacher in all cases. The only re-striction was that the aide was to stay within the limits of his (her) assigned group of students (even in regard to grad-ing papers).

At the end of the school year, the Stanford Early School Achievement Test was again administered in an identical manner to both classes. The results were tabulated and re-corded.

Method

Subjects

The subjects for this study were selected from the kindergarten population ($\underline{N}$ = 96) enrolled at an elementary school in Dade County, Florida. The school is located in a middle class, suburban neighborhood. The children who attend this school are predominantly Nonhispanic Caucasian. Fifty of the kindergarten children were randomly selected to participate in this study.

Instruments

The Metropolitan Readiness Tests (MRT), Form A, was selected and utilized as the posttest instrument. The MRT is designed to be administered to children at either the end of kindergarten or the beginning of the first grade. The subtests included in this battery are: Word Meaning, Listening, Matching, Alphabet, Numbers, Copying, and Draw-A-Man (optional). The battery provides eight scores, a score for each subtest and a total test score. The test is administered orally in 3 sessions, with a total testing time of 90 minutes. Reliability coefficients have been computed using both the split-half and alternate-forms techniques; they range from .90 to .95. The MRT was selected because it is a well constructed, valid, reliable instrument which met the requirements of the present study in that it was designed to measure the educational development of kindergarten students.

Experimental Design

The design utilized in this study was the posttest - only control group design (See Figure 1). This design was selected because of the feasibility of random selection and assignment, and the infeasibility of administering a pretest; readiness tests are generally intended to be administered at the end of kindergarten, not the beginning. This design does well in controlling for sources of internal and external validity; it does not, however, control for mortality. This potential threat to internal validity did not prove to be a problem, however, as group composition remained constant throughout the duration of the study.

Group	Selection/Assignment	Treatment	Posttest
1 ($\underline{n}$=25)	Random	Play-Oriented Curriculum	MRT[a]
2 ($\underline{n}$=25)	Random	Academic Readiness-Oriented Curriculum	MRT

[a] Metropolitan Readiness Tests

Figure 1. Experimental design.

Procedure

Prior to the beginning of the school year, in September, the 50 randomly selected kindergarten students were randomly assigned to one of two classes. The classes were then randomly designated experimental (play-oriented) or control (academic readiness-oriented). Parents of the 50 selected children were sent standard forms, provided by the school system, requesting permission for their children's participation in the study. All forms were returned and all the parents gave their permission.

All four kindergarten teachers expressed a willingness to be involved in the study. The two kindergarten teachers who were most alike with respect to education and experience were selected. Both teachers had graduate degrees in early childhood education; one of the teachers had 7 years experience, the other 10. Since neither teacher had any feelings one way or the other concerning the treatments, one was randomly designated to be the experimental class teacher. She was familiar with the concept of a play-oriented curriculum and required minimal training. Since the other teacher was to implement the usual curriculum, she required no training.

Treatment began at the end of the first week of school. The two classrooms were self-contained units and were as identical as possible. Both groups followed the same school schedule (8:15 - 2:00), and participated in the same extracurricular activities (e.g., plays, assemblies) provided by the school.

Subjects in the play-oriented group participated in a curriculum which emphasized the development of readiness skills and academic achievement by utilizing play activities and learning centers. The play-oriented curriculum was characterized as flexible, permitting the children time to explore the environment, manipulate concrete objects, experience and infer principles of learning, develop growth concepts and engage in social interaction with peers. The children were provided opportunities to engage in various categories of play: functional play, where the child exercised his/her muscles; constructive play, where the child manipulated objects to create objects or symbols; and dramatic play, where the child used language in order to imitate the role of a person. The teacher functioned as a facilitator of cognitive development.

Subjects in the academic readiness-oriented group participated in a curriculum which emphasized the development of readiness skills and cognitive abilities by utilizing teacher directed instruction and implementing commerically developed, highly structured approaches and materials. The academic readiness curriculum had distinct subject matter disciplines, and centered on large group instruction which held the students to long periods of controlled activities; activities were reinforced by the utilization of workbooks and worksheets.

At the end of May, Form A of the Metropolitan Readiness Tests was administered to all subjects. The subjects were administered on a group basis, in the classrooms, in three sessions, by the participating teachers; the teachers were assisted by trained paraprofessionals, one per classroom.

PART SEVEN

DATA ANALYSIS AND INTERPRETATION

EXERCISES

Exercise VII - 1 assesses your ability to select the appropriate statistic for a given research situation. Exercise VII - 2 assesses your ability to calculate the various statistics demonstrated in Part VII of the text. The suggested responses for this exercise show the steps involved in arriving at the final answer. Corresponding STATPAK printouts are also given for those of who will be using the software that accompanies the text. Following Exercise VII - 2, instructions for using STATPAK are presented. Use this exercise to check your ability to use STATPAK as well as your ability to correctly compute the statistics.

Read each of the descriptions following the list of inferential statistics. For each description, identify the appropriate statistic and place its letter on the blank in front of the description.

A   t test for independent samples
B   t test for nonindependent samples
C   simple analysis of variance
D   Scheffe' test
E   factorial analysis of variance
F   analysis of covariance
G   chi square

1. _____ Four randomly formed groups of n=20 each were administered a standardized reading achievement test as a posttest and F=7.42. You want to know if the performance of the three experimental groups is significantly greater than the performance of the control group.

2. _____ Four existing classes participated in an experimental math curriculum for eight months and four existing classes served as controls. You want to know if the computational skill of the experimental classes is significantly greater than the computational skill of the control classes. We have administered a standardized test of computational skill to all eight classes.

3. _____ Two randomly formed groups, one experimental and one control, have been administered a pretest and a posttest to measure comprehension of scientific principles. You want to statistically compare the posttest scores and we want to use the pretest scores to increase the power of the statistical test.

4. _____ One group of children classified as behavior problems has been involved in a systematic behavioral change program for one month. A second group of such children has not been involved in any special program. You want to statistically compare the frequency with which children in the two groups exhibit socially unacceptable behaviors.

5. _____ Two randomly formed groups will be asked to read a number of passages. One group will be taught strategies for remembering facts and concepts, the other group will not. At the end of the study both groups will be tested on the reading passages and the retention level of the groups will be compared.

The purpose of this exercise is to give you practice in calculating the various statistics. Perform the required operations yourself <u>before</u> checking the Suggested Responses. Double check all your figures. Students rarely have trouble with the statistical formulas; it is usually the arithmetic that hangs them up.

$$\underline{X}$$

2

4

4

5

6

6

6

7

8

9

_____

$\overline{X}$ =

<u>SD</u> =

$\underline{z}_1 =$

$\underline{z}_2 =$

$\underline{z}_3 =$

$\underline{z}_4 =$

$\underline{z}_5 =$

$\underline{z}_6 =$

$\underline{z}_7 =$

$\underline{z}_8 =$

$\underline{z}_9 =$

$\underline{z}_{10} =$

X	Y
2	6
4	6
4	7
5	8
6	9

$\underline{r}$ =

X_1	X_2	X_3
2	3	7
3	3	8
4	4	8
5	5	8
7	6	9

$\underline{t}$ test for independent samples ($\alpha = .05$)
for the X_1 and X_2 scores

$\underline{t}$ test for nonindependent samples $\quad (\alpha = .05)$
  for the X_2 and X_3 scores

Simple analysis of variance for 3 groups $(\alpha = .05)$
for the X, X_2 and X_3 scores

The Scheffé test $(\alpha = .05)$
for the $\overline{X}_1$ versus $\overline{X}_2$, $\overline{X}_2$ versus $\overline{X}_3$,
and $\overline{X}_1$ versus $\overline{X}_3$ comparisons

Chi Square -- χ^2 $(\alpha = .05)$

for the X, X_2 and X_3 sums

How to Use STATPAK

STATPAK is available in two versions, one for use with the Apple II family of micros and one for use with MS DOS (IBM compatible) computers. Your instructor will give you the disk that is appropriate for the hardware available to you.

The Apple disk is what is called a "flippy". The front of the disk is for use with an Apple IIe or Apple IIc. The back of the disk is for use with an Apple II or Apple II+. If you insert the disk and it doesn't work right, simply flip it over and use the other side.

The steps involved in using STATPAK with an Apple computer are as follows:

1. Insert the disk (with the appropriate side up) into Drive 1 and close the disk drive door.
2. Turn on the monitor (if necessary).
3. Turn on the computer.
4. Turn on the printer (if you have one and wish to make hardcopies).
5. The computer will "boot up" and load the program. When the program has been loaded, follow the directions printed on the screen.

The steps involved in using STATPAK with an MS DOS computer are as follows:

1. Insert the system disk which came with your computer into Drive A.
2. Turn on the monitor (if necessary).
3. Turn on the computer.
4. Turn on printer (if you have one and wish to make hardcopies).
5. The computer will "boot up" and may ask you for the date and the time. Respond by simply pressing the ENTER key until you have the prompt A> on your screen.
6. When you have the prompt A> remove the system disk and insert the STATPAK disk.
7. Type in STATPAK and press the ENTER key.
8. When the program has been loaded, follow the directions printed on the screen.

That's it! STATPAK is so user friendly, you could probably use it without further instruction. Just to be on the safe side, however, a basic overview of the program will be presented. One general procedure to note is that in order to move from screen to screen or to enter a response, you simply press the RETURN or ENTER Key. For example, if you select option 2, Pearson r, from the menu, simply type 2 and then press RETURN. If you are asked a yes-no question such as "Would you like a hardcopy?" type Y or N and press the RETURN or ENTER Key. If you make an inappropriate entry, the program will "trap" it, beep the speaker, and indicate the nature of your error.

STATPAK begins with screens that present information such as the name of the program and its author. Following the introductory information, the menu appears as follows:

Enter the number of your choice:
1. MEAN AND STANDARD DEVIATION
2. PEARSON r

3. z AND T Scores
4. t TEST FOR INDEPENDENT SAMPLES
5. t TEST FOR NONINDEPENDENT SAMPLES
6. ANOVA
7. CHI SQUARE
8. QUIT

You type the number of your choice and press RETURN. The program verifies your selection so that if you inadvertently type the wrong number, you are given an opportunity to make the correction. "Program Loading" then flashes on the screen, followed by a request for your data. For each statistic, you are given instructions for entering your data, and an opportunity to make corrections (in case you inadvertently enter one or more incorrect scores). Scores are entered one at a time; you type the first score and press RETURN, type the next score and press RETURN, and so on. (When you are asked by the program to put in an item, this means the same as score.) When you are through, you type END and press RETURN.

The program then computes the chosen statistic and asks you if you would like a hardcopy, i.e., if you would like the results printed out. You then respond Y (yes) or N (no) and press RETURN. If you enter N, results are displayed on the screen.

Note: If you enter Y and nothing happens, make sure the printer is on!

You are then asked if you would like to 1) run the same program again, or 2) return to STATPAK. If you chose 2, you go back to the menu. When you are completely finished, you type 8 (quit) and press RETURN. You then remove the disk, turn off the printer, and turn off the computer (turn off the monitor, if necessary).

The displayed or printed results for some of the statistics include one or more steps as well as the final answer. For example, in addition to the standard deviation (SD), you are also given the sum of the squared scores (EX^2). For other statistics (i.e. Pearson r, t test for nonindependent samples, ANOVA), you are simply given the correct answer, N, and df, and are given the option to check your work, i.e., to see the steps that contributed to the final answer. In both cases, the steps are available to you to assist you in locating errors if your answer is not very close (within rounding differences) of the answer given.

Note: E is used to represent Σ, and
R is used to represent r.

That's all there is to it. Whether this is your first experience using a micro or just your latest, you will appreciate just how user friendly STATPAK is. As always - trust me!

121

PART SEVEN

DATA ANALYSIS AND INTERPRETATION

TASK 7

Based on Tasks 2-6 which you have already completed,
write the results section of a research report.
Generate data for each of the subjects in your
study, summarize and describe the data using
descriptive statistics, statistically analyze
the data using inferential statistics, and
interpret the results in terms of your original
research hypothesis. Present the results of
your data analyses in a summary table.

Task 7 involves computation and interpretation of the descriptive and
inferential statistics which are appropriate given your research hypothesis.
The examples which follow were developed by the same students who prepared
the previous examples. Do not forget that while the examples represent the
performance required by Task 7, you must also submit the calculations involved in arriving at the figures which you will present in table form. The
calculations which were submitted for Task 7 are presented for the last example, Effects of a Play-Oriented Kindergarten Curriculum on Academic
Readiness.

The Effectiveness of the Use of Hand-Held

Calculators in Tenth Grade General Math Classes

Results

The Mathematics Computation section of the California Achievement Tests (Level 18C) was administered as the pretest to both the calculator and the noncalculator groups. Examination of the means as well as a t test for independent samples indicated that the groups were essentially equivalent (See Table 1). Special treatment was administered, as previously described, to the calculator group during an eight-month period and both groups were posttested using the same instrument used for the pretest. A t test for independent samples was used to compare the year-end achievement of the calculator and non-calculator groups. Random assignment of students into the groups made such a test appropriate. It was found that the two means differed significantly (See Table 1). Therefore, the original hypothesis that "tenth grade general mathematics students who are taught with hand-held calculators for an eight-month period show greater achievement on tests of computational skills (taken without the use of a calculator) than their peers who are taught without calculators" was supported.

Table 1

Means, Standard Deviations, and ts for the Calculator Group and the Noncalculator Group on the Pretest and Posttest

| | Group | | |
| | Calculator | Noncalculator | |
Test			t
Pretest			
M	21.6	21.2	$.41^a$
SD	2.47	2.69	
Posttest			
M	28.9	25.4	2.29^b
SD	4.00	4.10	

[a] $df = 58$, $p > .05$

[b] $df = 58$, $p < .05$

Behavior Modification as an Alternative

To Amphetamine Therapy in Treating

Hyperkinesis in Children

Results

Examination of pretest means indicated that the groups were essentially the same at the beginning of the study (See Table 1). Porteus Maze scores range from 0-20, with higher scores indicating higher levels of impulsivity and less ability to sustain attention. As Table 1 indicates, levels of hyperactivity were quite high in all three groups, with mean scores of 14.7, 14.9, and 15.2 respectively.

Table 1

Means and Standard Deviations for the Behavior Modification, Amphetamine Therapy, and Control Groups on the Pretest and Posttest

| | Group | | |
	Behavior Modification[a]	Amphetamine Therapy[a]	Control[a]
Pretest			
Mean	14.7	14.9	15.2
SD	3.1	2.7	2.8
Posttest			
Mean	6.8	6.7	14.8
SD	1.8	1.7	2.6

[a] $\underline{n}$ = 15

Following the five-month treatment period, the Porteus Maze Test was again administered to all subjects. The posttest scores of the three randomly formed groups were compared using a one-way analysis of variance. It was found that the groups differed significantly ($\underline{F}$ = 66.13, df = 2/42, $\underline{p}$ < .05). Application of the Scheffe test revealed that while the behavior modification and amphetamine therapy groups did not differ significantly (6.8 versus 6.7), both treatment groups did differ significantly from the control group (6.8 versus 14.8 and 6.7 versus 14.8). The control group maintained essentially the same level of hyperactivity during the five-month period (15.2 versus 14.8); the level of hyperactivity was reduced in both experimental groups, from 14.7 to 6.8 and from 14.9 to 6.7 (See Table 1). Thus, the original hypothesis that "behavior modification techniques will be as effective as amphetamines in reducing the hyperactivity of children in a classroom setting" was supported.

The Effectiveness of the Use of Preceptors

In the Orientation of New Graduate Nurses

Results

The Florida Medical Center Skills Inventory was administered to both the experimental (preceptor) group and the control group as a pretest. Inspection of the means indicated that as a result of random selection the groups were basically the same with respect to perceived initial level of skill. (See Table 1). At the conclusion of a 12-week orientation period, the Florida Medical Center Skills Inventory was administered as a posttest to each member of the experimental group and the control group. Since the groups were randomly formed, a t test for independent samples was used to compare the two groups on the results of the posttest. It was found that the groups differed significantly (See Table 1).

Table 1
Means, Standard Deviations, and t for the Experimental and Control Groups on the Pretest and Posttest

	Group		
Test	Preceptor	Traditional	t
Pretest			
M	66.0	67.0	
SD	8.2	8.1	
Posttest			
M	117.0	96.0	20.83[a]
SD	6.9	4.4	

[a]$\underline{df}$ = 50, $\underline{p}$ < .05

Therefore, the original hypothesis that "new graduate nurses whose orientation program utilizes a preceptor as a major component exhibit higher performance levels than new graduate nurses in a traditional orientation program" was supported.

The Comparative Effectiveness of Parent

Aides Versus Salaried Paraprofessionals

In the Kindergarten Classroom

Results

The Stanford Early School Achievement Test (Level 1) was administered as a pretest to both the parent and para-professional groups. Examination of the means indicated that the groups were essentially equivalent on the pretest measure at the beginning of the study (See Table 1). Treatment was administered to both groups during the nine-month school year and at the end of this period the Stanford Early School Achievement Test (Level 1) was administered again to both groups. A t test for independent samples was used to compare the achievement of the two groups. This statistical technique was employed because the groups were independent of each other, i.e., subjects were randomly assigned to either the parent group or the paraprofessional group. It was found that the two means did not differ significantly (See Table 1).

Therefore, the original hypothesis that "kindergarten students who have a volunteer parent pool assisting their teacher in the classroom will show comparable achievement to kindergarten students who have a salaried paraprofessional in their classroom" was supported.

Table 1

Means, Standard Deviations and t for the Parent Group and the Paraprofessional Group on the Pretest and Posttest

| Test | Group | | t |
	Parent	Paraprofessional	
Pretest			
Mean	51.15	50.40	
SD	14.33	13.56	
Posttest			
Mean	72.21	70.47	.51[a]
SD	15.06	14.42	

[a] $df = 58$, $p > .05$

Effects of a Play-Oriented Kindergarten
Curriculum on Academic Readiness

Results

A t test for independent samples was utilized to compare the posttest
achievement of the treatment group and the control group. Random assignment
of students into the groups made it appropriate to employ this statistical
technique. It was found that the two means differed significantly (see
Table 1). Therefore, the original hypothesis that "kindergarten children
who participate in a play-oriented curriculum will exhibit greater academic
readiness skills at the end of kindergarten than kindergarten children who
participate in an academic readiness-oriented curriculum" was supported.

Table 1

Posttest Means, Standard Deviations, and t for the Play-Oriented and Academic
Readiness-Oriented Curriculum Groups

| | Group | | |
	Play-Oriented Curriculum	Academic Readiness-Oriented Curriculum	t
M	41.33	36.20	2.68[a]
SD	5.88	4.52	

[a]df = 48, p < .05

	Experimental			Control	
	X_1	X_1^2		X_2	X_2^2
1	30	900		29	841
2	34	1,156		30	900
3	36	1,296		31	961
4	37	1,369		33	1,089
5	38	1,444		33	1,089
6	38	1,444		34	1,156
7	39	1,521		35	1,225
8	42	1,764		36	1,296
9	43	1,849		38	1,444
10	45	2,025		38	1,444
11	46	2,116		39	1,521
12	46	2,116		40	1,600
13	47	2,209		42	1,764
14	49	2,401		42	1,764
15	50	2,500		43	1,849
	620	26,110		543	19,943
	EX_1	EX_1^2		EX_2	EX_2^2

$$\overline{X}_1 = 41.33$$

$$\overline{X}_2 = 36.20$$

---

[1]Since the purpose of Task 7 is for the student to learn how to apply and interpret statistics, when student studies involve large n's some instructors allow their students to perform the actual calculations on a smaller number of scores, usually n = 15 per group, and to write Task 7 as if the results were based on the actual n. If necessary, consult with your instructor to see if this approach is acceptable.

Standard Deviations

Experimental

$$SD = \sqrt{\frac{SS}{N-1}}$$

$$SS = EX^2 - \frac{(EX)^2}{N}$$

$$SS = 26,110 - \frac{(620)^2}{15}$$

$$= 26,110 - \frac{384,400}{15}$$

$$= 26,110 - 25,626.67$$

$$= 483.33$$

$$SD = \sqrt{\frac{483.33}{14}}$$

$$= \sqrt{34.523571}$$

$$= 5.88$$

Control

$$SD = \sqrt{\frac{SS}{N-1}}$$

$$SS = EX^2 - \frac{(EX)^2}{N}$$

$$SS = 19,943 - \frac{(543)^2}{15}$$

$$= 19,943 - \frac{294,849}{15}$$

$$= 19,943 - 19,656.60$$

$$= 286.40$$

$$SD = \sqrt{\frac{286.40}{14}}$$

$$= \sqrt{20.457142}$$

$$= 4.52$$

t Test

$$t = \frac{\overline{X}_1 - \overline{X}_2}{\sqrt{\left(\frac{SS_1 + SS_2}{n_1 + n_2 - 2}\right)\left(\frac{1}{n_1} + \frac{1}{n_2}\right)}}$$

$$= \frac{41.33 - 36.20}{\sqrt{\left(\frac{483.33 + 286.40}{15 + 15 - 2}\right)\left(\frac{1}{15} + \frac{1}{15}\right)}}$$

$$= \frac{5.13}{\sqrt{\left(\frac{769.73}{28}\right)\left(\frac{2}{15}\right)}}$$

$$= \frac{5.13}{\sqrt{(27.4904)\ (.1333)}}$$

$$\frac{5.13}{\sqrt{3.6645}} = \frac{5.13}{1.91} = 2.68$$

$$t = 2.68,\ \underline{df} = 28,\ \alpha = .05$$

table value = 2.048   2.68 > 2.048

131

---------------------------------------   ---------- ---. -------------------------

THE NUMBER OF SCORES (N) IS 15   THE NUMBER OF SCORES (N) IS 15

THE SUM OF THE SCORES (EX) IS 620   THE SUM OF THE SCORES (EX) IS 543

THE MEAN OF THE SCORES ($\overline{X}$) IS 41.33   THE MEAN OF THE SCORES ($\overline{X}$) IS 36.2

THE SUM OF THE SQUARED SCORES (EX^2)   THE SUM OF THE SQUARED SCORES (EX^2)
IS 26110   IS 19943

THE SUM OF SQUARES (SS) IS 483.33   THE SUM OF SQUARES (SS) IS 286.4

THE STANDARD DEVIATION FOR A   THE STANDARD DEVIATION FOR A
SAMPLE IS 5.88   SAMPLE IS 4.52

THE STANDARD DEVIATION FOR A   THE STANDARD DEVIATION FOR A
POPULATION IS 5.68   POPULATION IS 4.37

---------------------------------------   ---------------------------------------

```
FOR THE TEST ONE VS TWO.
=========================================
N OF ONE = 15
SUM OF SCORES = 620
MEAN = 41.33
SUM OF SQUARED SCORES = 26110
THE 'SS' OF ONE = 483.33

N OF TWO = 15
SUM OF SCORES = 543
MEAN = 36.2
SUM OF SQUARED SCORES = 19943
THE 'SS' OF TWO = 286.4

THE t VALUE IS 2.68
THE DEGREES OF FREEDOM ARE 28
=========================================
```

PART EIGHT

RESEARCH REPORTS

TASK 8

   Based on Tasks 2, 6, and 7, prepare a research report
which follows the general format for a thesis or
dissertation.

   Task 8 entails combining Tasks 2, 6, and 7, preparing preliminary pages
(including an abstract), and adding a discussion section. Since Task 8 is
relatively straightforward, only one example which illustrates the performance called for will be presented. This example represents the synthesis of
the previously presented tasks related to the effects of a play-oriented
kindergarten curriculum.

Effects of a Play-Oriented Kindergarten

Curriculum on Academic Readiness

Deborah G. Lane

College of Education, Florida International University

Task 8

Submitted in partial fulfillment of

the requirements for EDF 5481

December, 1985

Table of Contents

(i)

---

[1]Example page numbers are in parentheses to differentiate them from the page numbers of this book.

List of Tables

(ii)

136

List of Figures

.

(iii)

Abstract

The purpose of this study was to investigate the comparative effectiveness of a play-oriented kindergarten curriculum versus an academic readiness-oriented kindergarten curriculum. Using a posttest-only control group design and the t test for independent samples, it was found that after approximately eight months the play-oriented group achieved significantly higher scores on the Metropolitan Readiness Tests, Form A, than the academic readiness-oriented group $[t(48) = 2.68, p < 05]$. It was concluded that the play-oriented curriculum was more effective in faciliting academic readiness skills.

(iv)

Introduction[1]

In recent years, an emphasis has been placed on academic achievement, cognitive learning, and preparation for the next grade level. Following the Russian launching of Sputnik, the public concluded that American schools had failed, and the question "What are we teaching our children?" was generated (Gallegos, 1983; Webster, 1984). This question placed great pressure on school systems to develop curricula which would accelerate the child's academic training and skills, with kindergarten becoming the first front in this "academic war".

As a result, no longer are kindergarteners allowed to merely interact with their peers and to explore the educational environment and the learning process. Rather, these five-year-olds are now receiving formal instruction, especially in the area of reading, from commercially produced structured programs and materials. Today's kindergarteners are expected to complete worksheets and participate in phonics lessons, and are held to long periods of controlled activities. These children participate in an academically oriented routine that was once expected of first graders (Ballenger, 1983; Gentile & Hoot, 1983).

For many educators, the issue is not whether these young children can be successfully taught, but rather whether this structured approach is truly beneficial to them. Many believe that kindergarteners were, in fact, better prepared for academic pursuits when they were allowed time to acquire judgment of symbols, develop a pattern of exploration, explore their environment, and experiment without risk of failure (Ballenger, 1983).

Statement of Problem

The purpose of this study was to compare the effects of two curriculum models, a play-oriented curriculum and an academic readiness-oriented curriculum, with respect to the academic readiness of kindergarteners. A play-oriented curriculum was defined as a "curriculum emphasizing child-directed representations of symbols through activities in which constructive materials, imaginative sequences, and elements of language are used" (Wolfgang & Sanders, 1981). An academic readiness-oriented curriculum was defined as a highly structured curriculum stressing phonics instruction and utilization of workbooks.

Review of Related Literature

The academic readiness programs which are found in American kindergartens today have multiplied during the past two decades. This increase has come about because of the desire of educators, and society in general, to improve children's opportunities for academic success (May & Campbell, 1981). The concept of these readiness programs evolved during the 1920's and 1930's in an attempt to reduce the number of failures in the first and second grades. However, today the term readiness is not accepted by all educators. Some find the term too vague, while others feel that programs

(1)

---

[1]Theses and dissertations are generally double-spaced. This example is not, in the interest of textbook length.

have become too rigid (May & Campbell, 1981), and view them as unwise attempts to accelerate the child's academic training and achievement (Johnson & Johnson, 1982).

Critics of academic readiness programs question whether five- or six-year-olds are cognitively ready for the complex decoding and abstracting processes required in learning how to read. Their criticism is based on research findings which conclude that it is not until the age of seven or eight that children develop the logical thinking ability which is essential in giving meaning to the written word (Johnson & Johnson, 1982). In addition, many educators perceive this type of early childhood program as an extension of the elementary school, where kindergarteners begin to receive formalized reading instruction which was once reserved for first graders (Elkind, 1982; Webster, 1984). Studies concerned with the optimal age at which early instruction should begin, early reading instruction in particular, have been conducted (Elkind, 1982). According to Johnson and Johnson (1982), a study conducted by Davis, Timble, and Vincent found that children who started first grade at the age of six registered significantly higher scores on reading achievement tests than those who started at the age of five. A similar finding was reported by Feitelson, Tehori, and Levinberg-Green (1982), who worked with five- to seven-year-olds in Israel. These researchers reported that children who entered first grade at the age of six-and-one-half years or older scored significantly higher than those students who entered first grade at age six or younger. Other researchers have also questioned the value of early academic training because it does not appear to provide any permanent advantage to those young children who receive it (Davis, 1980; Johnson & Johnson, 1982; Webster, 1984).

Furthermore, in terms of academic learning from a Plagetian view, a child can not begin to comprehend reading material unless it reflects the child's existing knowledge. This knowledge must have been constructed from personal experiences with objects and through a variety of play activities (Raph, 1980). According to May and Campbell (1981), Maier states that Piaget stresses a number of developmental levels which the child must experience in order for learning to take place. If educators attempt to escalate learning without taking into account the child's developmental levels, it could result in the child's first learning experience being one of frustration. This may in turn cause children to associate future learning with frustration, something to be avoided (Davis, 1980; Gallegos, 1983).

A number of educators and psychologists do not necessarily disagree with the above, but believe that learning can be accelerated if instruction is appropriate to the child's level. They cite Bruner and his associates who claim that any subject can be taught to any child at any stage of development (Johnson & Johnson, 1982); May & Campbell, 1981). It is these educators and psychologists who have dominated the early childhood education movement. Based on their assertions, society has pressured schools into establishing structured reading programs for early childhood classes. These societal pressures evolved from over-anxious parents, administrators who have little or no academic training in early childhood education, and publishers with powerful salesmanship qualities (Davis, 1980; Elkind, 1982). In their zest to teach kindergarten children to read by mandating large segments of teaching time, and by requiring kindergarten teachers to use highly structured reading programs and materials, these parents and

(2)

educators have failed to realize how this instruction severely limits the opportunities for these five-year-olds to engage in play activities which are also a vital part of learning (Gentile & Hoot, 1983).

Recent expansion of research in the area of play and its effects on learning firmly supports the theories that claim that there is a critical relationship among play, learning to read, and early reading achievement (Gentile & Hoot, 1983). According to Pellegrini (1980), Glickman, in an attempt to explain reasons for young children's declining achievement scores, hypothesized that this decline may be due to a decrease in the frequency and quality of children's play at both home and school. Based on the results of his research, Glickman found a positive relationship between preschoolers' ability to play and performance on cognitive achievement tests. To further develop Glickman's research, Pellegrini (1980) conducted a study on school-age children which resulted in similar findings. In addition, Gallegos (1983) conducted a study of kindergarteners in which half of the children were enrolled in classes that stressed learning through play activities, and half were enrolled in classes that emphasized learning through teacher-directed instruction. This study also generated data supporting the premise that play does have a significant influence on the mastery of academic readiness skills. Further, the study found that the play group exhibited additional growth gains over and above the direct instruction group in a majority of the performance areas.

Statement of the Hypothesis

Most of the research on kindergarten curricula has focused on reading instruction and achievement. The research has generally found that delaying formal instruction is more productive. Other research has demonstrated the positive effects of play on achievement, and there is some evidence that play is more effective than structured activities. Given the evidence for reading, and the absence of contradictory findings in other curriculum areas, it is hypothesized that kindergarten children who participate in a play-oriented curriculum will exhibit greater academic readiness skills at the end of kindergarten than kindergarten children who participate in an academic readiness-oriented curriculum.

(3)

Method

Subjects

The subjects for this study were selected from the kindergarten population (N = 96) enrolled at an elementary school in Dade County, Florida. The school is located in a middle class, suburban neighborhood. The children who attend this school are predominantly Nonhispanic Caucasian. Fifty of the kindergarten children were randomly selected to participate in this study.

Instrument

The Metropolitan Readiness Tests (MRT), Form A, was selected and utilized as the posttest instrument. The MRT is designed to be administered to children at either the end of kindergarten or the beginning of the first grade. The subtests included in this battery are: Word Meaning, Listening, Matching, Alphabet, Numbers, Copying, and Draw-A-Man (optional). The battery provides eight scores, a score for each subtest and a total test score. The test is administered orally in 3 sessions, with a total testing time of 90 minutes. Reliability coefficients have been computed using both the split-half and alternate-forms techniques; they range from .90 to .95. The MRT was selected because it is a well constructed, valid, reliable instrument which met the requirements of the present study in that it was designed to measure the educational development of kindergarten students.

Experimental Design

The design utilized in this study was the posttest only control group design (See Figure 1). This design was selected because of the feasibility of random selection and assignment, and the infeasibility of administering a pretest; readiness tests are generally intended to be administered at the end of kindergarten, not the beginning. This design does well in controlling for sources of internal and external validity; it does not, however, control for mortality. This potential threat to internal validity did not prove to be a problem, however, as group composition remained constant throughout the duration of the study.

Group	Selection/Assignment	Treatment	Posttest
1 (n=25)	Random	Play-Oriented Curriculum	MRT[a]
2 (n=25)	Random	Academic Readiness-Oriented Curriculum	MRT

[a]Metropolitan Readiness Tests

Figure 1. Experimental design.   (4)

142

Procedure

Prior to the beginning of the school year, in September, the 50 randomly selected kindergarten students were randomly assigned to one of two classes. The classes were then randomly designated experimental (play-oriented) or control (academic readiness-oriented). Parents of the 50 selected children were sent standard forms, provided by the school system, requesting permission for their children's participation in the study. All forms were returned, and all the parents gave their permission.

All four kindergarten teachers expressed a willingness to be involved in the study. The two kindergarten teachers who were most alike with respect to education and experience were selected. Both teachers had graduate degrees in early childhood education; one of the teachers had 7 years experience, the other 10. Since neither teacher had any feelings one way or the other concerning the treatments, one was randomly designated to be the experimental class teacher. She was familiar with the concept of a play-oriented curriculum and required minimal training. Since the other teacher was to implement the usual curriculum, she required no training.

Treatment began at the end of the first week of school. The two classrooms were self-contained units and were as identical as possible. Both groups followed the same school schedule (8:15 - 2:00), and participated in the same extracurricular activities (e.g., plays, assemblies) provided by the school.

Subjects in the play-oriented group participated in a curriculum which emphasized the development of readiness skills and academic achievement by utilizing play activities and learning centers. The play-oriented curriculum was characterized as flexible, permitting the children time to explore the environment, manipulate concrete objects, experience and infer principles of learning, develop growth concepts and engage in social interaction with peers. The children were provided opportunities to engage in various categories of play: functional play, where the child exercised his/her muscles; constructive play, where the child manipulated objects to create objects or symbols; and dramatic play, where the child used language in order to imitate the role of a person. The teacher functioned as facilitator of cognitive development.

Subjects in the academic readiness-oriented group participated in a curriculum which emphasized the development of readiness skills and cognitive abilities by utilizing teacher directed instruction and implementing commercially developed, highly structured approaches and materials. The academic readiness curriculum had distinct subject matter disciplines, and centered on large group instruction which held the students to long periods of controlled activities; activities were reinforced by the utilization of workbooks and worksheets.

At the end of May, Form A of the Metropolitan Readiness Tests was administered to all subjects. The subtests were administered on a group basis, in the classrooms, in three sessions, by the participating teachers; the teachers were assisted by trained paraprofessionals, one per classroom.

(5)

Results

A t test for independent samples was utilized to compare the posttest achievement of the treatment group and the control group. Random assignment of students into the groups made it appropriate to employ this statistical technique. It was found that the two means differed significantly (see Table 1). Therefore, the original hypothesis that "kindergarten children who participate in a play-oriented curriculum will exhibit greater academic readiness skills at the end of kindergarten than kindergarten children who participate in an academic readiness-oriented curriculum" was supported.

Table 1

Posttest Means, Standard Deviations, and t for the Play-Oriented and Academic Readiness-Oriented Curriculum Groups.

	Group		
Test	Play-Oriented Curriculum	Academic Readiness-Oriented Curriculum	t
M	41.33	36.20	2.68[a]
SD	5.88	4.52	

[a]df = 48, p < .05

(6)

Discussion

Based on the aforementioned results, it was concluded that the play-oriented curriculum had a significant impact on the achievement of the academic readiness skills of the kindergarten children. Thus, the original hypothesis, that kindergarten children who participate in a play-oriented curriculum will exhibit greater academic readiness skills at the end of kindergarten than kindergarten children who participate in an academic readiness-oriented curriculum, was supported.

However, since this study utilized two classrooms of 25 middle-class kindergarten children, and teachers with graduate degrees in early childhood education, results cannot be generalized to all classroom environments, with varying backgrounds of children, and diverse educational levels of teachers. In view of the results, it would appear that educational research should continue to investigate the effects of play on cognitive development. This continued research should evaluate the effects of play on disparate kindergarten children and teachers. It may be, for example, that play is even more beneficial for lower-class children, whose home environments tend to be less educationally stimulating.

Kindergarten children are experts at play. It is incumbent upon educators to capitalize on this fact and to utlize play activities to enhance academic readiness skills in particular, and general cognitive development in general.

(7)

References

Ballenger, M. (1983). Reading in Kindergarten. Childhood Education, 59, 186-187.

Davis, H. (1980). Reading pressures in the kindergarten. Childhood Education, 57, 76-79.

Elkind, D. (1982). Early education: Are young children exploited? A commentary on Feitelson, Tehori, and Levinberg-Green. Merrill-Palmer Quarterly, 28, 495-497.

Feitelson, D., Tehori, B. Z., & Levinberg-Green, D. How effective is early instruction in reading? Experimental evidence. Merrill-Palmer Quarterly, 28, 485-493.

Gallegos, M. (1983). Learning Academic skills through play. (ERIC Document Reproduction Service No. ED 225 690)

Gentile, F. M., & Hoot, J. L. (1983). Kindergarten play: the foundation of reading. The Reading Teacher, 36, 436-439.

Johnson, B., & Johnson, C. (1982). Overplacement: Children to failure. USA Today, 110(2442), 52-54.

May, C. R., & Campbell, R. (1981). Readiness for learning: Assumptions and realities. Theory Into Practice, 20, 130-134.

Pellegrini, A. D. (1980). The relationship between kindergarteners' play and achievement in prereading language and writing. Psychology in the Schools, 17, 530-535.

Raph, J. B. (1980). A cognitive start in kindergarten: Theory-research review. (ERIC Document Reproduction Service No. ED 194 188)

Webster, N. K. (1984). The 5s and 6s go to school, revisited. Childhood Education, 60, 325-330.

Wolfgang, C. H., & Sanders, T. S. (1981). Defending young children's play as the ladder to literacy. Theory Into Practice, 20, 116-120.

(8)

PART NINE

RESEARCH CRITIQUES

TASK 9

> Given a reprint of a research report and an evaluation
> form, evaluate the components of the report.

Task 9 entails application of a number of questions to the evaluation of an actual research report. In order to give you practice in evaluating a research study, one of the reports presented in Part One, Effects of Goal Setting on Achievement in Archery, has been evaluated for you. Following this discussion, questions are listed for you to answer with respect to that article. In answering the questions, use the following codes:

Y = Yes

N = No

? = Cannot tell (it cannot be determined from the
information given)

NA = Question not applicable

X = Given your current level of competence, you are
not in a position to make a judgment.

When appropriate, as you answer the questions, underline components which correspond to questions to which you have responded "Y". For example, if ou decide that there is a statement of the problem, underline it in the article. Since the study which you are going to evaluate is experimental, you are also asked to identify and diagram the experimental design used. If your responses match reasonably well with those given in the Suggested Responses, you are probably ready for Task 9. Make sure that you understand the reason for any discrepancies, especially on questions for which responses are less judgmental and more objective; adequacy of the literature review is more judgmental whereas the presence or absence of a hypothesis can be objectively determined.

Effects of Goal Setting on

Achievement in Archery

GENERAL EVALUATION CRITERIA

Introduction

Problem   CODE

    Is there a statement of the problem?

    Is the problem "researchable"?   ____

    Is background information on the problem
        presented?   ____

    Is the educational significance of the
        problem discussed?   ____

    Does the problem statement indicate the
        variables of interest and the specific
        relationship between those variables
        which was investigated?   ____

    When necessary, are variables directly
        or operationally defined?   ____

Review of Related Literature

    Is the review comprehensive?   ____

    Are all references cited relevant to
        the problem under investigation?   ____

    Are the sources mostly primary or were
        a number of secondary sources cited?   ____

    Have references been critically analyzed
        and the results of various studies
        compared and contrasted or is the
        review basically a series of ab-
        stracts or annotations?   ____

    Is the review well-organized, does it
        logically flow in such a way that
        the references least related to the
        problem are discussed first and the
        most related references are dis-
        cussed last?   ____

    Does the review conclude with a brief
        summary of the literature and its
        implications for the problem investi-
        gated?   ____

    Do the implications discussed form an
        empirical or theoretical rationale
        for the hypotheses which follow?   ____

Hypotheses

Are specific questions to be answered
   listed or specific hypotheses to
   be tested stated? _____

Does each hypothesis state an expected
   relationship or difference between
   two variables? _____

If necessary, are variables directly or
   operationally defined? _____

Is each hypothesis testable? _____

Method

Subjects

Are the size and major characteristics of
   the population studied described? _____

Was the entire population studied? _____

Was a sample selected? _____

Is the method of selecting a sample
   clearly described? _____

Is the method of sample selection
   described one that is likely to
   result in a representative, un-
   biased sample? _____

Were volunteers used? _____

Are the size and major characteristics
   of the sample described? _____

Does the sample size meet the suggested
   guideline for minimum sample size
   appropriate for the method of research represented? _____

Instruments

Is a rationale given for selection of
   the instruments used? _____

Is each instrument described in terms
   of purpose and content? _____

Are the instruments appropriate for
   measuring the intended variables? _____

If an instrument was developed specifically
   for the study, are the procedures
   involved in its development and
   validation described? _____

Is evidence presented that indicates
   that each instrument is appropriate
   for the sample under study? _____

Is instrument validity discussed and
    coefficients given if appropriate? _____

Is reliability discussed in terms of type
    and size of reliability coefficients? _____

If appropriate, are subtest reliabilities
    given? _____

If an instrument was specifically developed
    for the study, are administration,
    scoring, and interpretation procedures
    fully described? _____

Design and Procedure

Is the design appropriate for testing the
    hypotheses of the study? _____

Are procedures described in sufficient
    detail to permit them to be replicated
    by another researcher? _____

Was a pilot study conducted? _____

If a pilot study was conducted are its
    execution and results described, as
    well as its impact on the subsequent
    study? _____

Are control procedures described? _____

Are there any potentially confounding
    variables which were not controlled? _____

Results

Are appropriate descriptive statistics
    presented? _____

Was the probability level, p, at which
    the results of the tests of sig-
    nificance were evaluated, specified
    in advance of data analysis? _____

If parametric tests were used is there
    any evidence that one or more of
    the required assumptions were
    greatly violated? _____

Are the tests of significance described
    appropriate, given the hypotheses
    and design of the study? _____

Was every hypothesis tested? _____

Are the tests of significance interpreted
    using the appropriate degrees of
    freedom? _____

Are the results clearly presented? _____

Are the tables and figures (if any) well
    organized and easy to understand? _____

Are the data in each table and figure
    described in the text? _____

Conclusions and Recommendations

Is each result discussed in terms of the
original hypothesis to which it
relates?

Is each result discussed in terms of its
agreement or disagreement with previous results obtained by other researchers in other studies?

Are generalizations made that are not
warranted by the results?

Are the possible effects of uncontrolled
variables on the results discussed?

Are theoretical and practical implications of the findings discussed?

Are recommendations for future action
made?

Based only on statistical significance,
are suggestions for educational action
made that are not justified by the
data; in other words, has the author
confused statistical significance
and practical significance?

Are recommendations for future research
made?

Summary (Or Abstract)

Is the problem restated?

Are the number and type of subjects
and instruments described?

Is the design used identified?

Are procedures described?

Are the major results and conclusions
restated?

METHOD-SPECIFIC EVALUATION CRITERIA

Identify and diagram the experimental
design used in this study:

Was an appropriate experimental design
selected?

Is a rationale for design selection given?

Are sources of invalidity associated
with the design identified and
discussed?

Is the method of group formation
described?

Was the experimental group formed in the same way as the control group? _____

Were existing groups used or were groups randomly formed? _____

Were treatments randomly assigned to groups? _____

Were critical extraneous variables identified? _____

Were any control procedures applied to equate groups on extraneous variables? _____

Is there any evidence to suggest reactive arrangements (for example, the Hawthorne effect)? _____

SUGGESTED RESPONSES

PART ONE

SELF-TEST FOR TASK 1-A

Meaning as a Factor in Predicting Spelling Difficulty

The Problem.   The purpose of the study was to determine whether or not understanding the meanings of words uniquely contributes to their "spellability," after the effects of word frequency, word length and phoneme-grapheme regularity have been statistically partialed out (neutralized).

The Procedures. One hundred words were randomly selected from The Teacher's Word Book of 30,000 Words. Frequency of occurrence in written materials, number of letters (length), and an index of phoneme-grapheme regularity were calculated for each of the 100 words. The list of 100 words was broken down into sublists of 25 words each. For each set of words, an oral-dictation-in-context spelling test and a multiple-choice vocabulary test were developed. The tests were administered on four consecutive days to 180 white middle-class 4th, 6th, and 8th graders of mixed ability levels.

The Method of Analysis. Partial correlation coefficients were calculated between spelling difficulty (SD) and each of the predictor variables, holding all other variables constant. Separate multiple regressions were also done using spelling and vocabulary data obtained from subjects at each level.

The Major Conclusion. There is a relationship between the spelling difficulty of a word and knowledge of the word's meaning.

The Effect of Male Teachers on the Academic
Achievement of Father-Absent Sixth Grade Boys

The Problem. This study investigated the effects of male teachers on the academic achievement of father-absent sixth grade boys.

The Procedures. In a large midwestern city, 193 boys on whom there were complete data were identified from school records as being father absent. Of these, 90 had been assigned to 40 male teachers during their sixth grade year and 103 had been assigned to 46 female teachers, all in essentially self-contained classrooms. Five total subtest scores from the Iowa Tests of Basic Skills (ITBS) - Vocabulary, Reading Comprehension, Language, Work Study, and Mathematics - served as both the pretest and posttest measures, having been administered in April of the fifth and sixth grade years. Intelligence quotients were from the total score of the Short Form Test of Academic Aptitude, which had been administered in April of the boys' fifth grade year.

The Method of Analysis. t - test comparisons between the two groups were made on the five criterion measures of the ITBS, intelligence quotients, and chronological age. Subsequently, analysis of covariance with I.Q. and fifth grade ITBS scores as covariates was used to analyze the data.

The Major Conclusion. There was no evidence that assignment of father-absent boys to male teachers, in and of itself, was able to enhance the academic achievement of these sixth grade boys.

Prestigious Psycho-Educational Research Published From 1910 to 1974: Types of Explanations, Focus, Authorship, and Other Concerns

The Problem. This review is an attempt systematically to describe prestigious psycho-educational research published in selected journals from the first date of their publication to recent times. Unlike other reviews, which are topically focused, this review is focused on such concerns as the types of explanations generated, number and types of subjects, patterns of topics, and funding and institutional affiliations of authors.

The Procedures. Articles in the sample were drawn on the basis of half-decade periods beginning in 1910. Computerized random numbers were generated to first select a volume of each journal and then an article from that volume. Three articles per half decade, per journal, were selected. The journals began publication at different times, so thirty-nine Journal of Educational Psychology (JEP), six American Educational Research Journal (AERJ), and thirty-three Journal of Educational Research (JER) articles were analyzed. Two judges independently selected the explanatory statements of each article from its summary or conclusion. Using Brown's types, two judges independently categorized the explanatory statements into one of the categories and discussed to concensus the fifteen cases of disagreement.

The Method of Analysis. The data were presented by decade and journal in a table in terms of frequency counts of type of explanation, type of study, and focus on achievement.

The Major Conclusions. Empirical generalizations were more typical of experimental studies than either descriptive or intentional-dispositional explanations, whereas descriptive and intentional-dispositional explanations were more frequently used in nonexperimental studies. Studies during 1950 and after included more empirical generalizations and fewer of the other types of explanations than studies through 1949. Though there were more experimental studies and fewer nonexperimental studies in the more recent period, the difference is not great. The majority of studies over the period focused on achievement.

Effects of Goal Setting on Achievement in Archery

The Problem. The purpose of the research was to study the relationship of specific participative goal setting to achievement in archery over the regularly scheduled 10-week instructional period.

The Procedures. Wayne State University undergraduates enrolled in 3 beginning archery classes were randomly assigned to one of two groups - group conference with goal setting (N=18) or group conference only (N=12). Subjects in the group conference with goal setting group were directed to set individual verbal and numerical goals at the end of each weekly 10-minute conference period using a printed goal-setting sheet. The conference-only group met weekly for 10 minutes with the instructor and discussed problem areas in the skill of archery. All subjects participated in the 10 week instructional unit on archery. Subjects were tested three times (on an initial test, a progress test and a final achievement test) while shooting from a distance of 20 yards.

The Method of Analysis. Analysis of the performance score data was completed using a split-plot analysis of covariance (ANCOVA) with initial test performance scores used as a covariate for the between-subject effect.

The Major Conclusion. Participative goal setting can be effective in promoting increased achievement in a motor skill - archery - when utilized over a 10-week instructional period.

Basic Concepts in the Oral Directions of Group Achievement Tests

The Problem. The purpose of this study is to answer the following question: Are basic concepts included in the teacher's oral directions of commonly used group achievement tests? Basic concepts are defined as those most frequently misunderstood by primary level children and included in the Boehm Test of Basic Concepts.

The Procedures. The following primary level group achievement tests were screened for basic concepts within the teacher's oral directions: California Achievement Tests, Iowa Tests of Basic Skills, Metropolitan Achievement Tests, and the Stanford Diagnostic Reading Test.

The Method of Analysis. Only teacher's directions intended to orient students to the task demands were included in the analyses. For each subtest, Boehm's basic concepts appearing in these directions were identified and listed.

The Major Conclusions. Boehm's basic concepts are frequently used in the teacher's oral directions to subtests. The construct validity of a subtest that purports to assess abilities other than language is questionable when basic concepts are used in the oral directions.

Testing Versus Review: Effects on Retention

The Problem. The purpose of this study was to answer the following question: Is spending some portion of a teaching session in testing really more valuable than spending the same time in further study? By addressing this question, the authors were comparing the consolidation hypothesis with the total-time hypothesis.

The Procedures: Ninety-seven senior students from a suburban middle-class high school participated in this experiment. The students were randomly assigned to three groups, two experimental and one control, and all were asked to read and study a brief history passage. Immediately afterward, the first group was tested on the passage (students received no feedback); the second group reviewed the passage for an equal amount of time; the third group performed a "filler" task for an equal amount of time. A retention task on the passage was given to all students two weeks later. The initial test given to the first group contained 12 questions, half multiple-choice and half short-answer. The retention test given 2 weeks later to all students contained 24 questions, half multiple-choice and half short answer.

The Method of Analysis. Analysis of variance was performed on scores followed by planned contrasts.

The Major Conclusion. The results of the study indicate that testing is indeed more profitable for retention. Although review itself was profitable, as indicated by a sample increase of 10% in retention over control group performance, testing was even more profitable (resulting in a sample increase of 25% over control group performance).

SELF-TEST FOR TASK 1-B

Meaning as a Factor in Predicting Spelling Difficulty

Method: Correlational

Reasons: A cause-effect relationship was <u>not</u> investigated. A relationship was investigated - the relationship between the spelling difficulty of a word and knowledge of the word's meaning. Correlation coefficients were computed.

The Effect of Male Teachers on the Academic
Achievement of Father-Absent Sixth Grade Boys

Method: Causal-Comparative

Reasons: A cause-effect relationship was investigated. The independent variable (cause), sex of teacher (male versus female) was not manipulated. Subjects were selected who <u>had been taught</u> by either a male teacher or a female teacher. The subjects' scores on five subtests of the <u>Iowa Tests of Basic Skills</u> were then compared.

Prestigious Psycho-Educational Research Published
From 1910 to 1974: Types of Explanations, Focus,
Authorship, and Other Concerns

Method: Historical

Reasons: This research involved the study and analysis of past events. It was concerned with describing the nature of published psycho-educational research articles and looking for differences between those published prior to 1950 and those published during and after 1950.

Effects of Goal Setting on Achievement in Archery

Method: Experimental

Reasons: A cause-effect relationship was investigated. The independent
           variable (cause) goal setting (individual goal setting at weekly
           conferences versus converences only), was manipulated. Subjects
           were randomly assigned to the goal-setting conference group or the
           conference only group. The subjects' performance on a series of
           archery tests was then compared.

          ⨯ Basic Concepts in the Oral Directions of
                 Group Achievement Tests

Method: Descriptive

Reasons: This study was designed to answer the question "are basic concepts
           included in the teacher's oral directions of commonly used group
           achievement tests?" Commonly used tests were examined and basic
           concepts were identified in the directions and listed.

          Testing Versus Review: Effects on Retention

Method: Experimental

Reasons: A cause-effect relationship was investigated. The independent
           variable (cause), activity following instruction (testing versus
           review versus "filler"), was manipulated. Subjects were randomly
           assigned to a testing group, a review group, or a control group.
           The subjects' performance on a retention test was compared.

PART TWO

EXERCISE II - 1

1. Hyperactive primary-level children who receive diet therapy exhibit more
    on-task behavior than hyperactive primary-level children who receive
    drug therapy.
2. College-level introductory psychology students who take short-answer
    tests have greater retention of psychological concepts and principles
    than college-level introductory psychology students who take multiple-
    choice tests.
3. Public school students who graduate have higher incomes at age 25 than
    public school students who drop out of school prior to graduation.
4. Junior high school students who receive positive verbal reinforcement
    are absent less frequently than junior high school students who receive
    negative verbal reinforcement.

5. Upper elementary students who participate in computer-assisted drill and practice show greater achievement on tests of computational skill than upper elementary students who participate in teacher-directed drill and practice.

EXERCISE II - 2

1. There is no difference in the on-task behavior of hyperactive primary-level children who receive diet therapy and those who receive drug therapy.
2. There is no difference in the retention of psychological concepts and principles of college-level introductory psychology students who take short-answer tests and those who take multiple-choice tests.
3. There is no difference in the income at age 25 of public school students who graduate and those who drop out prior to graduation.
4. There is no difference in the frequency of absenteeism of junior high school students who receive positive verbal reinforcement and those who receive negative verbal reinforcement.
5. There is no difference in the computational skill of upper elementary students who participate in computer-assisted drill and practice and those who participate in teacher-directed drill and practice.

PART FOUR

EXERCISE IV - 1

1. There are 150 first graders in the population and you want a random sample of 60 students.

    1) Compile or obtain a list of the 150 first graders.
    2) Assign each subject a number from 000-149.
    3) Go to a table of random numbers and arbitrarily select a number.
    4) Look at the last 3 digits of the numbers.
    5) If that number is also assigned to a subject, that subject is in the sample; if not, go to the next number.
    6) Continue down the table until 60 students are selected.

2. There are 220 principals in the school system and you want a random sample of 40 principals.

    1) Compile or obtain a list of the 220 principals.
    2) Assign each principal a number from 000-219.
    3) Go to a table of random number and arbitrarily select a number.
    4) Look at the last 3 digits of the number.
    5) If that number is also assigned to a subject, that subject is in the sample; if not go to the next number.
    6) Continue down the table until 40 principals are selected.

3. There are 320 students defined as gifted in the school system and you want a random sample of 50 gifted students.

    1) Compile or obtain a list of the 320 gifted students.
    2) Assign each gifted student a number from 000-319.
    3) Go to a table of random numbers and arbitrarily select a number.
    4) Look at the last 3 digits of the number.
    5) If that number is also assigned to a subject, that subject is in the sample; if not go to the next number.
    6) Continue down the table until 50 gifted students are selected.

1. There are 500 twelfth-grade students in the population, you want a sample of 60 students, and you want to stratify on three levels of IQ in order to insure equal representation.

    1) Administer an IQ test (or otherwise obtain IQ scores) and classify all students into one of three IQ groups (e.g., those with an IQ below 84, those with IQ between 84 and 116, and those with an IQ above 116).

    2) Randomly select 20 students from each IQ group.

2. There are 95 algebra I students in the population, you want a sample of 30 students, and you want to stratify a sex in order to insure equal representation of males and females.

    1) Classify all the algebra I students as male or as female.

    2) Randomly select 15 males and 15 females.

3. There are 240 principals in the school system, you want a sample of 45 principals, and you want to stratify by level, i.e., elementary versus secondary, in order to insure proportional representation. You know that there are approximately twice as many secondary principals as elementary principals.

    1) Identify all the elementary principals and all the secondary principals.

    2) Randomly select 15 elementary principals and 30 secondary principals; this will give you a sample of 45 which contains twice as many secondary principals as elementary principals.

EXERCISE IV - 3

1. There are 80 sixth-grade classrooms in the population, each classroom has an average of 30 students, and you want a sample of 180 students.

    1) The number of classrooms needed $= \dfrac{180}{30} = 6$.

    2) Randomly select 6 classrooms from the population of 80 classrooms.

3) All the sixth graders in the 6 classrooms selected are in the sample.

2. There are 75 schools in the school system, each school has an average of 50 teachers, and you want a sample of 350 teachers.

   1) The number of schools needed = $\frac{350}{50}$ = 7.

   2) Randomly select 7 schools from the population of 75 schools.
   3) All the teachers in the 7 schools selected are in the sample.

3. There are 100 kindergarten classes in the school system, each class has an average of 20 children, and you want a sample of 200 children.

   1) The number of kindergarten classes needed = $\frac{200}{20}$ = 10.

   2) Randomly select 10 kindergartens from the population of 100 kindergarten classes.
   3) All the children in the 10 classes selected are in the sample.

EXERCISE IV - 4

1. You have a list of 2,000 high school students and you want a sample of 200 students.

   1) K = $\frac{2,000}{200}$ = 10.

   2) Arbitrarily select a name at the top of the list.
   3) Select every 10th name on the list until you have selected 200 students.

2. You have a directory which lists the names and addresses of 12,000 teachers and you want a sample of 2,500 teachers.

   1) K = $\frac{12,000}{2,500}$ = 4.8 or 5.

   2) Arbitrarily select a name at the beginning of the directory.

3) Select every 5th name in the directory until you have selected 2,500 teachers.

3. You have a list of 1,500 junior high school students and you want a sample of 100 students.

1) $K = \dfrac{1,500}{100} = 15.$

2) Arbitrarily select a name at the top of the list.
3) Select every 15th name until you have selected 100 students.

_____

PART FIVE

EXERCISE V - 1

1. A   2. D   3. C   4. A   5. B

EXERCISE V - 2

1. C   2. A   3. B   4. B   5. C

EXERCISE V - 3

1. You want to determine the concurrent validity of a new IQ test for young children.

   1) Obtain scores on an already established, valid IQ test for a large group of young children (or administer such a test if scores are not already available).
   2) Administer the new IQ test to the same group.
   3) Correlate the two sets of scores.
   4) If the correlation is high, the new test has high concurrent validity with the already established test.

2. You want to determine the concurrent validity of a new self-concept scale for junior high school students.

   1) Obtain scores on an already established, valid self-concept scale for a large group of junior high school students (or administer such a test if scores are not already available).
   2) Administer the new self-concept scale to the same group.
   3) Correlate the two sets of scores.
   4) If the correlation is high, the new scale has high concurrent validity with the already established scale.

3. You want to determine the concurrent validity of a new reading comprehension test for high school students.

   1) Obtain scores on an already established, valid test of reading comprehension for a large group of high school students (or administer such a test if scores are not already available).
   2) Administer the new reading comprehension test to the same group.
   3) Correlate the two sets of scores.
   4) If the correlation is high, the new scale has high concurrent validity with the already established test.

1. You want to predict success in graduate school and you want to determine the predictive validity of the GRE.

   1) Administer the GRE to a large group of students entering graduate school.
   2) Collect data on the criterion measure, a valid index of success in graduate school such as GPA at the time of graduation.
   3) Correlate the two sets of data.
   4) If the correlation is high, the GRE has high predictive validity with respect to success in graduate school.

2. You want to predict level of achievement in algebra I and you want to determine the predictive validity of an algebra I aptitude test.

   1) Administer the algebra aptitude test to a large group of students who are going to take algebra I.
   2) Collect data on the criterion measure, a valid index of level of achievement in algebra I such as final exam scores or final average.
   3) Correlate the two sets of data.
   4) If the correlation is high, the algebra I aptitude test has high predictive validity with respect to level of achievement in algebra I.

3. You want to predict success in nursing school and you want to determine the predictive validity of a nursing aptitude test.

   1) Administer the nursing aptitude test to a large group of students who are entering nursing school.
   2) Collect data on the criterion measure, a valid index of success in nursing school such as scores on a final performance test.
   3) Correlate the two sets of scores.
   4) If the correlation is high, the nursing aptitude test has high predictive validity with respect to success in nursing school.

EXERCISE VI - 1

| 1. G | 2. L | 3. A | 4. E | 5. C |

EXERCISE VI - 2

| 1. G | 2. G | 3. A | 4. C | 5. B |

EXERCISE VII - 1

1. D   2. B   3. F   4. G   5. A

EXERCISE VII - 2

X	X^2
2	4
4	16
4	16
5	25
6	36
6	36
6	36
7	49
8	64
9	81
$\sum X = 57$	$\sum X^2 = 363$

$$\overline{X} = \frac{\sum X}{N} = \frac{57}{10} = \underline{\underline{5.7}}$$

$$SD = \sqrt{\frac{\sum X^2 - \frac{(\sum X)^2}{N}}{N-1}} = \sqrt{\frac{363 - \frac{(57)^2}{10}}{9}} = \sqrt{\frac{363 - \frac{3249}{10}}{9}}$$

$$= \sqrt{\frac{363 - 324.9}{9}} = \sqrt{\frac{38.1}{9}} = \sqrt{4.23} = \underline{\underline{2.06}}$$

$\underline{X}$	$\underline{Y}$	$\underline{X^2}$	$\underline{Y^2}$	$\underline{XY}$
2	6	4	36	12
4	6	16	36	24
4	7	16	49	28
5	8	25	64	40
6	9	36	81	54
21	36	97	266	158
$\sum X$	$\sum Y$	$\sum X^2$	$\sum Y^2$	$\sum XY$

$$r = \frac{\sum XY - \frac{(\sum X)(\sum Y)}{N}}{\sqrt{\left[\sum X^2 - \frac{(\sum X)^2}{N}\right]\left[\sum Y^2 - \frac{(\sum Y)^2}{N}\right]}} = \frac{158 - \frac{(21)(36)}{5}}{\sqrt{\left[97 - \frac{(21)^2}{5}\right]\left[266 - \frac{(36)^2}{5}\right]}}$$

$$= \frac{158 - \frac{756}{5}}{\sqrt{\left[97 - \frac{441}{5}\right]\left[266 - \frac{(1296)}{5}\right]}} = \frac{158 - 151.2}{\sqrt{\left[97 - 88.2\right]\left[266 - 259.2\right]}}$$

$$= \frac{6.8}{\sqrt{\left[8.8\right]\left[6.8\right]}} = \frac{6.8}{\sqrt{59.84}} = \frac{6.8}{7.74} = .8786$$

$$\underline{r} = \underline{\underline{.88}}$$

$$\underline{z}_1 = \frac{X - \overline{X}}{SD} = \frac{2 - 5.7}{2.06}$$

$$= \frac{-3.7}{2.06} = \underline{\underline{-1.80}}$$

$$\underline{z}_2 = \frac{X - \overline{X}}{SD} = \frac{4 - 5.7}{2.06}$$

$$= \frac{-1.7}{2.06} = \underline{\underline{-.83}}$$

$$\underline{z}_3 = \frac{X - \overline{X}}{SD} = \frac{4 - 5.7}{2.06}$$

$$= \frac{-1.7}{2.06} = \underline{\underline{-.83}}$$

$$\underline{z}_4 = \frac{X - \overline{X}}{SD} = \frac{5 - 5.7}{2.06}$$

$$= \frac{-.7}{2.06} = \underline{\underline{-.34}}$$

$$\underline{z}_5 = \frac{X - \overline{X}}{SD} = \frac{6 - 5.7}{2.06}$$

$$\frac{.3}{2.06} = \underline{\underline{+.15}}$$

$$\underline{z}_6 = \frac{X - \overline{X}}{SD} = \frac{6 - 5.7}{2.06}$$

$$= \frac{.3}{2.06} = \underline{\underline{+.15}}$$

$$\underline{z}_7 = \frac{X - \overline{X}}{SD} = \frac{6 - 5.7}{2.06}$$

$$= \frac{.3}{2.06} = \underline{\underline{+.15}}$$

$$\underline{z}_8 = \frac{X - \overline{X}}{SD} = \frac{7 - 5.7}{2.06}$$

$$= \frac{1.3}{2.06} = \underline{\underline{+.63}}$$

$$\underline{z}_9 = \frac{X - \overline{X}}{SD} = \frac{8 - 5.7}{2.06}$$

$$= \frac{2.3}{2.06} = \underline{\underline{+1.12}}$$

$$\underline{z}_{10} = \frac{X - \overline{X}}{SD} = \frac{9 - 5.7}{2.06}$$

$$= \frac{3.3}{2.06} = \underline{\underline{+1.60}}$$

X_1	X_2	X_3
2	3	7
3	3	8
4	4	8
5	5	8
7	6	9

$\underline{t}$ test for independent samples

x_1	x_1^2	x_2	x_2^2
2	4	3	9
3	9	3	9
4	16	4	16
5	25	5	25
7	49	6	36
21	103	21	95
Σx_1	Σx_1^2	Σx_2	Σx_2^2

$$\overline{X}_1 = \frac{\Sigma x_1}{n_1} = \frac{21}{5} = 4.2 \qquad \overline{X}_2 = \frac{\Sigma x_2}{n_2} = \frac{21}{5} = 4.2$$

$$SS_1 = \Sigma x_1^2 - \frac{(\Sigma x_1)^2}{n_1} \qquad\qquad SS_2 = \Sigma x_2^2 - \frac{(\Sigma x_2)^2}{n_2}$$

$$= 103 - \frac{(21)^2}{5} \qquad\qquad\qquad = 95 - \frac{(21)^2}{5}$$

$$= 103 - \frac{441}{5} \qquad\qquad\qquad\quad = 95 - \frac{441}{5}$$

$$= 103 - 88.2 \qquad\qquad\qquad\quad = 95 - 88.2$$

$$= 14.8 \qquad\qquad\qquad\qquad\quad = 6.8$$

$$\underline{t} = \frac{\overline{X}_1 - \overline{X}_2}{\sqrt{\left(\dfrac{SS_1 + SS_2}{n_1 + n_2 - 2}\right)\left(\dfrac{1}{n_1} + \dfrac{1}{n_2}\right)}} = \frac{4.2 - 4.2}{\sqrt{\left(\dfrac{14.8 + 6.8}{5 + 5 - 2}\right)\left(\dfrac{1}{5} + \dfrac{1}{5}\right)}}$$

$$= \frac{0}{\sqrt{\left(\dfrac{21.6}{8}\right)\left(\dfrac{2}{5}\right)}} = \frac{0}{\sqrt{\left(2.7\right)\left(.4\right)}} = \frac{0}{\sqrt{1.08}} = \frac{0}{1.04} = 0$$

$\underline{t} = 0$

$\underline{df} = n_1 + n_2 - 2 = 5 + 5 - 2 = 8$

$\alpha = .05$

$\underline{t} = 0$ is less than 2.306 (See Table A.4)

Therefore, there is no significant difference between the two groups.

$\underline{t}$ test for nonindependent samples

$\underline{X_2}$	$\underline{X_3}$	$\underline{D}$	$\underline{D^2}$
3	7	+4	16
3	8	+5	25
4	8	+4	16
5	8	+3	9
6	9	+3	9

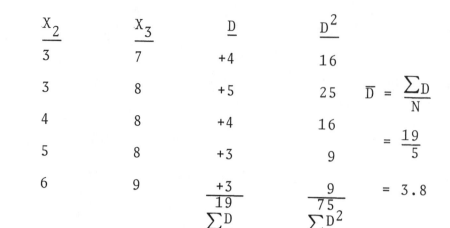

$$\overline{D} = \frac{\sum D}{N}$$

$$= \frac{19}{5}$$

$$= 3.8$$

$$\frac{+3}{19}\ \underset{\sum D}{} \qquad \frac{9}{75}\ \underset{\sum D^2}{}$$

$$\underline{t} = \frac{\overline{D}}{\sqrt{\dfrac{\sum D^2 - \dfrac{(\sum D)^2}{N}}{N(N-1)}}} \qquad = \frac{3.8}{\sqrt{\dfrac{75 - \dfrac{(19)^2}{5}}{5(5-1)}}}$$

$$= \frac{3.8}{\sqrt{\dfrac{75 - \dfrac{361}{5}}{5(4)}}} \qquad = \frac{3.8}{\sqrt{\dfrac{75 - 72.2}{20}}} \qquad = \frac{3.8}{\sqrt{\dfrac{2.8}{2.0}}}$$

$$= \frac{3.8}{\sqrt{.14}} \qquad = \frac{3.8}{.37} \qquad = 10.27$$

$\underline{t} = 10.27$; $\underline{df} = n - 1 = 5 - 1 = 4$; $\alpha = .05$

$\underline{t} = 10.27$ is greater than 2.776 (See Table A.4)

Therefore, there is a significant difference between the two groups.

Simple analysis of variance for 3 groups

X_1	X_1^2	X_2	X_2^2	X_3	X_3^2
2	4	3	9	7	49
3	9	3	9	8	64
4	16	4	16	8	64
5	25	5	25	8	64
$\frac{7}{21}$	$\frac{49}{103}$	$\frac{6}{21}$	$\frac{36}{95}$	$\frac{9}{40}$	$\frac{81}{322}$
$\sum X_1$	$\sum X_1^2$	$\sum X_2$	$\sum X_2^2$	$\sum X_3$	$\sum X_3^2$

$$SS_{total} = SS_{between} + SS_{within}$$

$$SS_{between} = \frac{(\sum X_1)^2}{n_1} + \frac{(\sum X_2)^2}{n_2} + \frac{(\sum X_3)^2}{n_3} - \frac{(\sum X)^2}{N}$$

$$= \frac{(21)^2}{5} + \frac{(21)^2}{5} + \frac{(40)^2}{5} - \frac{(82)^2}{15}$$

$$= \frac{441}{5} + \frac{441}{5} + \frac{1,600}{5} - \frac{6,724}{15}$$

$$= 88.2 + 88.2 + 320 - 448.27$$

$$= 496.4 - 448.27 = \underline{48.13}$$

$$SS_{total} = \sum X^2 - \frac{(\sum X)^2}{N} = 520 - 448.27 = \underline{71.73}$$

$$SS_{within} = SS_{total} - SS_{between}$$

$$= 71.73 - 48.13 = \underline{23.60}$$

SOURCE OF VARIATION	SUM OF SQUARES	df		MEAN SQUARES	F
Between	48.13	(K-1)	2	24.06	12.21
Within	23.60	(N-K)	12	1.97	
Total	71.73	(N-1)	14		

F = 12.21; df = 2, 12; α = .05

F = 12.21 is greater than 3.88 (See Table A.5)

Therefore, there is a significant difference among the groups.

$$\overline{X}_1 = \frac{\mathcal{E}^{X_1}}{n} = \frac{21}{5} = 4.2$$

$$\overline{X}_2 = \frac{\mathcal{E}^{X_2}}{n_2} = \frac{21}{5} = 4.2$$

$$\overline{X}_3 = \frac{\mathcal{E}^{X_3}}{n_3} = \frac{40}{5} = 8.0$$

$$MS_w = 1.97$$

$$(K-1) = 3-1 = 2 \qquad\qquad (N-K) = 15-3 = 12$$

$$\underline{F} = \frac{(\overline{X}_1 - \overline{X}_2)^2}{MS_w \left(\frac{1}{n_1} + \frac{1}{n_2}\right)(K-1)} = \frac{0^2}{1.97\ (.4)2} = \frac{0}{1.58} = 0$$

$\underline{F} = 0$, $\underline{df} = 2, 12$, $\underline{p} = .05$, table value = 3.88

$\quad$ $0 < 3.88$, therefore there is no significant difference between $\overline{X}_1$ and $\overline{X}_2$

$$\underline{F} = \frac{(\overline{X}_2 - \overline{X}_3)^2}{MS_w\left(\frac{1}{n_1} + \frac{1}{n_2}\right)(K-1)} = \frac{(4.2 - 8.0)^2}{1.97\left(\frac{1}{5} + \frac{1}{5}\right)2}$$

$$= \frac{(-3.8)^2}{1.97\ (.4)2}$$

$$= \frac{14.44}{1.58}$$

$$= 9.14$$

$\underline{F} = 9.14$, $\underline{df} = 2.12$, $\alpha = .05$, table value = 3.88

$\quad$ $9.14 \quad 3.88$, therefore there $\underline{is}$ a significant difference between $\overline{X}_2$ and $\overline{X}_3$

Since $\overline{X}_1 = \overline{X}_2$, the calculations for $\overline{X}_1 - \overline{X}_3$ are the same as for $\overline{X}_2 - \overline{X}_3$

Chi square χ^2

Responses

	Yes	No	Undecided	
observed	21	21	40	total: 82
expected	27.3	27.3	27.3	

(Note: expected $= \dfrac{82}{3} = 27.3$)

$$\chi^2 = \sum \left[\frac{(fo - fe)^2}{fe} \right]$$

$$\chi^2 = \frac{(21 - 27.3)^2}{27.3} + \frac{(21 - 27.3)^2}{27.3} + \frac{(40 - 27.3)^2}{27.3}$$

$$= \frac{(-6.3)^2}{27.3} + \frac{(-6.3)^2}{27.3} + \frac{(12.7)^2}{27.3}$$

$$= \frac{39.69}{27.3} + \frac{39.69}{27.3} + \frac{161.29}{27.3}$$

$$= 1.45 + 1.45 + 5.91 = \underline{8.81}$$

$\chi^2 = 8.81$; $\underline{df} = K - 1 = 3 - 1 = 2$; $\alpha = .05$

$\chi^2 = 8.81 > 5.991$ (See Table A.6)

Therefore, there is a significant difference between observed and expected frequencies.

THE NUMBER OF SCORES (N) IS 10

THE SUM OF THE SCORES (EX) IS 57

THE MEAN OF THE SCORES ($\overline{X}$) IS 5.7

THE SUM OF THE SQUARED SCORES (EX^2) IS 363

THE SUM OF SQUARES (SS) IS 38.1

THE STANDARD DEVIATION FOR A SAMPLE IS 2.06

THE STANDARD DEVIATION FOR A POPULATION IS 1.95

THERE WERE 5 PAIRS OF SCORES.

THE PEARSON'S 'r' IS .88

THERE WERE 3 DEGREES OF FREEDOM

THESE ARE THE SCORES YOU ENTERED FOR X.

1 = 2
2 = 4
3 = 4
4 = 5
5 = 6

THESE ARE THE SCORES YOU ENTERED FOR Y.

1 = 6
2 = 6
3 = 7
4 = 8
5 = 9

EX = 21   EY = 36

EX^2 = 97 EY^2 = 266

EXY = 158   N = 5

$$EXY - \frac{(EX)(EY)}{N} = 6.8$$

LOWER LEFT BRACKETS

$$EX^2 - \frac{(EX)^2}{N} = 8.8$$

LOWER RIGHT BRACKETS

$$EY^2 - \frac{(EY)^2}{N} = 6.8$$

8.8 TIMES 6.8 = 59.84

THE SQUARE ROOT OF 59.84 = 7.74

$$r = \frac{6.8}{7.74} = .88$$

DEGREES OF FREEDOM ARE

N - 2 = DF

5 - 2 = 3

THE NUMBER OF SCORES (N) IS 10.

THE MEAN OF THE SCORES ($\bar{X}$) IS 5.7.

THE SD FOR A POPULATION IS 1.95.

THE SD FOR A SAMPLE IS 2.06.

SCORE	z-SCORE	Z OR T-SCORE
2	-1.8	32
4	-.83	41.7
4	-.83	41.7
5	-.34	46.6
6	.15	51.5
6	.15	51.5
6	.15	51.5
7	.63	56.3
8	1.12	61.2
9	1.6	66

FOR THE TEST ONE VS TWO.
==

N OF ONE = 5
SUM OF SCORES = 21
MEAN = 4.2
SUM OF SQUARED SCORES = 103
THE 'SS' OF ONE = 14.8

N OF TWO = 5
SUM OF SCORES = 21
MEAN = 4.2
SUM OF SQUARED SCORES = 95
THE 'SS' OF TWO = 6.8

THE t VALUE IS 0
THE DEGREES OF FREEDOM ARE 8
==

THE N IS 5

THE t VALUE IS 10.1559

THERE ARE 4 DEGREES OF FREEDOM

$\bar{D} = 3.8$

$ED^2 = 75$

$ED = 19$

$N = 5$

$$\frac{ED^2 - \frac{(ED)^2}{N}}{N(N-1)} = .14$$

$$\sqrt{.14} = .3742$$

$$\frac{3.8}{.3742} = 10.1559$$

YOU ENTERED THE FOLLOWING SCORES IN

GROUP ONE:

2, 3, 4, 5, 7,

YOU ENTERED THE FOLLOWING SCORES IN

GROUP TWO:

3, 3, 4, 5, 6,

YOU ENTERED THE FOLLOWING SCORES IN

GROUP THREE:

7, 8, 8, 8, 9,

GROUP	NO. SCORES	SUM OF SCORES	SUM OF SQUARED SCORES
ONE	5	21	103
TWO	5	21	95
THREE	5	40	322

SUMS OF SCORES

$SS_T = 71.73$

$SS_B = 48.13$

$SS_W = 23.6$

```
SOURCE      SUM
  OF         OF              MEAN
VARIATION  SQUARES      DF  SQUARE
========================================

BETWEEN    48.13    (K-1) 2   24.07
WITHIN     23.6     (N-K) 12  1.97

----------------------------------------

   TOTAL   71.73    (N-1) 14  F=12.24


----------------------------------------
              SCHEFFE TESTS
----------------------------------------

COMPARISON              F-RATIO
----------------------------------------

ONE VS TWO              0
ONE VS THREE            9.18
TWO VS THREE            9.18
ONE VS TWO & THREE      3.06

----------------------------------------
```

X^2 FOR CATEGORY 1= 1.45

X^2 FOR CATEGORY 2= 1.45

X^2 FOR CATEGORY 3= 5.91

X^2 = 8.81

THERE ARE 2 DEGREES OF FREEDOM.

PART NINE

SELF-TEST FOR TASK 9

Effects of Goal Setting on
Achievement in Archery

GENERAL EVALUATION CRITERIA

Introduction

Problem

	CODE
A Statement ?	Y

Implicity in paragraph (//) 1, sentence (S) 1
and // 3, S 1;Explicitly, // 5

Researchable?	Y
Background information?	Y

e.g. // 2

Significance discussed?	Y

e.g. // 3, S 1 & 2

Variables and relationships stated?	Y
Definitions?	N

Implied, but not directly stated.

Review of Related Literature

Comprehensive?	Y
References relevant?	Y
Sources primary?	Y
Critical analysis	Y

e.g. // 3, S 6 - 10.

Well organized?	Y
Summary?	N
Rationale for hypotheses?	NA

Hypotheses

Questions or hypotheses?	N
Expected difference stated?	NA
Variables defined?	NA
Testable?	NA

Note: Since the answer to the first question is N, the remainder of the
questions become NA.

Method

Subjects

Population described?	N
Entire population used?	?
Sample selected?	?
Method described?	N
Sample representative?	?
Volunteers?	N
Sample described?	N

     It is only stated what kinds of students were used;
     under Procedure, // 1, S 1.

Minimum size?	N

$$\underline{n}_1 = 18, \quad \underline{n}_2 = 12$$

Instruments

Rationale for selection?	NA

     Apparently a self-developed procedure was used;
     under Procedures, // 4, S 2.

Instruments described?	N
Appropriate?	?
Procedures for development described?	N
Evidence that appropriate for sample?	N
Validity discussed?	N
Reliability discussed?	N
Subtest reliabilities?	NA
Administration, scoring and interpretation procedures described?	N

Design and Procedure

Design appropriate?	Y
Procedures sufficiently detailed?	Y
Pilot study?	N
Description of pilot study?	NA
Control procedures described?	N
Confounding variables not controlled?	?

     Possible Hawthorne effect, for example

Results

Appropriate descriptive statistics?	Y
Probability level specified in advance?	?
Parametric assumptions violated?	X
Tests of significance appropriate?	X

     Also, since there is no hypothesis it is difficult to tell.

	CODE
Appropriate degrees of freedom?	X
Results clearly presented?	Y
Tables and figures well organized?	Y
Data in each table and figure described?	Y

Conclusions and Recommendations

	CODE
Results discussed in terms of hypotheses?	NA
Results discussed in terms of previous research?	Y
Next to last //, S 2	
Unwarranted generalizations?	N
Effects of uncontrolled variables discussed?	N
Implications discussed?	Y
Next to last //	
Recommendations for action?	N
Not directly state; implied under Results and Discussion, // 3	
Confusion of practical and statistical significance?	N
Recommendations for research?	Y
Last //	

Summary (or Abstract)

	CODE
Problem restated?	Y
Subjects and instrument described?	Y
Design identified?	Y
Procedures?	Y
Results and conclusions?	Y

METHOD-SPECIFIC EVALUATION CRITERIA

Design used:

Basically a pretest-posttest control group design with the addition of a progress test.

R O_1 X O_2 X O_3

R O_1 O_2 O_3

X = goal setting
O_1 = initial test
O_2 = progress test
O_3 = final test

	CODE
Design appropriate?	Y
Selection rationale?	N
Invalidity discussed?	N
Group formation described?	Y
Under Procedures, // 1, S 1	
Groups formed in same way?	Y
Groups randomly formed?	Y
Treatments randomly assigned?	O
Extraneous variables described?	N
Groups equated?	Y
Covariance was used to equate groups on initial performance level (under Results and Discussion, // 1, S 1)	
Reactive arrangements?	?
Possible Hawthorne effect, for example	